EVERYTHING YOU NEED TO KNOW ABOUT DINOSAURS

KINGFISHER
LONDON & NEW YORK

Copyright © Kingfisher 2012
Published in the United States by Kingfisher,
175 Fifth Ave., New York, NY 10010
Kingfisher is an imprint of Macmillan Children's Books, London.

Distributed in the U.S. and Canada by Macmillan,
175 Fifth Ave., New York, NY 10010

Written by Dougal Dixon and Margaret Hynes
Consultant: David Burnie

Library of Congress Cataloging-in-Publication data has been applied for.

ISBN: 978-0-7534-6831-9

Kingfisher books are available for special promotions and premiums.
For details contact: Special Markets Department, Macmillan,
175 Fifth Ave., New York, NY 10010.

For more information, please visit www.kingfisherbooks.com

Printed in China
9 8 7 6 5 4 3 2 1
1TR/0512/WKT/UG/140MA

NOTE TO READERS
The website addresses listed in this book are correct at the time of going to print. However, due to the ever-changing nature of the Internet, website addresses and content can change. Websites can contain links that are unsuitable for children. The publisher cannot be held responsible for changes in website addresses or content or for information obtained through third-party websites. We strongly advise that Internet searches should be supervised by an adult.

EVERYTHING YOU NEED TO KNOW ABOUT DINOSAURS

Dougal Dixon

KINGFISHER

NEW YORK

Contents

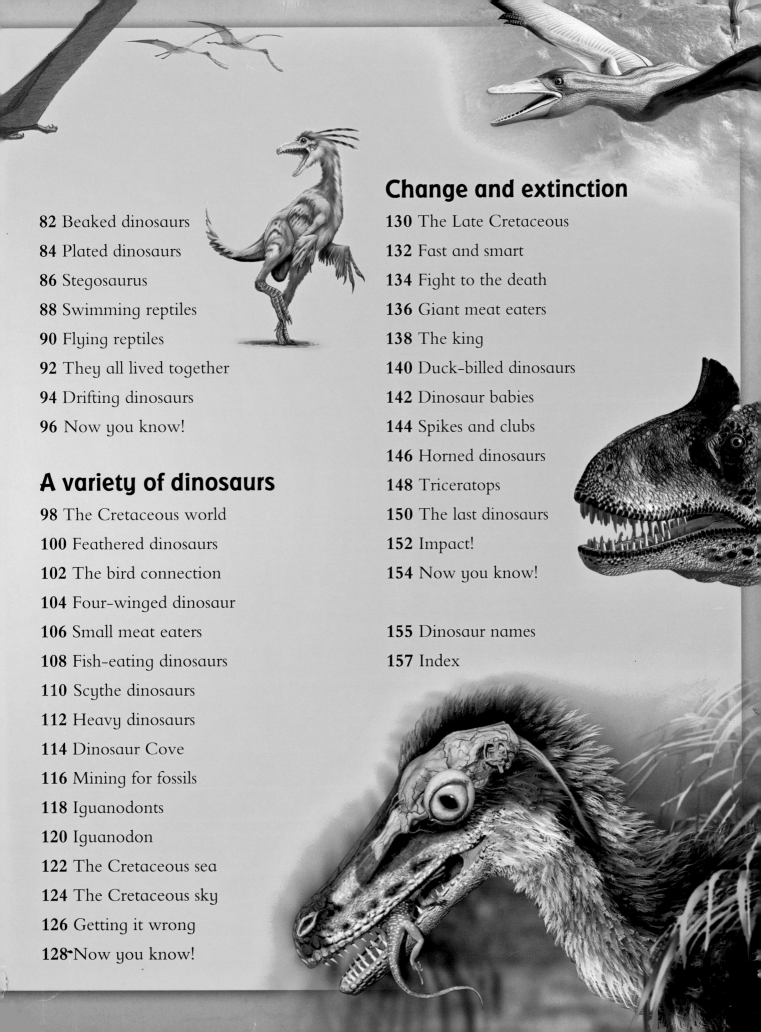

Using this book

As well as a lot of information, this book has many fun ideas in it to help you enjoy it more. There are facts to amaze you, vocabulary notepads to explain words, important questions with fascinating answers, and great activities. Enjoy exploring the world of dinosaurs!

► Amazing facts

Look out for the exclamation point on these boxes. Each "Amazing!" box contains an extraordinary fact. This "Amazing!" box is from the chapter called "Early dinosaurs." You will find it on page 19.

AMAZING!

Herrerasaurus and Eoraptor could stand almost upright and run on legs that were straight below their bodies. Most other reptiles in the Triassic had legs that sprawled out to the side.

JURASSIC PARK

Dinosaur movies and cartoons often get the facts wrong. In the movie "Jurassic Park," for example, Dilophosaurus had a neck frill and was able to spit poison. Neither of these things was true in real life.

◄ Fact box

Look out for these boxes with pictures. You can find interesting, in-depth information about dinosaurs in these boxes. This fact box is from the chapter called "A world of dinosaurs." You will find it on page 63.

► Vocabulary notepad

Sometimes difficult words that are used in the text need further explanation, so there is a notepad specially for this task. This "Vocabulary" notepad is from the chapter called "Change and extinction." You will find it on page 142.

VOCABULARY

colony
Animals of the same type living closely together.

reproduce
To have babies, or young animals.

WHICH SAUROPOD WAS THE BIGGEST?
We think Amphicoelias was the longest, but we know this dinosaur from one vertebra. The largest complete skeletons are Brachiosaurus and Diplodocus.

◄ Question circle

Everyone has questions they really want to ask. You will find circles with questions and their answers in every chapter. This "question" circle is from the chapter called "Giant dinosaurs." You will find it on page 77.

► Can you find?

These features will test what you can spot and name in the pictures. This footprint-shaped "Can you find?" is from "A variety of dinosaurs." You will find it on page 98.

CAN YOU FIND?
1. A dinosaur with a sail on its back
2. A large crocodile
3. A flying reptile

► Creative corner

The blobs of paint say it all! This is where you can let your creative self run wild. The book is packed with fun experiments and great things to make and do. This "Creative corner" is from "Giant dinosaurs." You will find it on page 71.

Creative corner

Hollow and solid bone test

(1) Make a solid "bone" by packing a toilet paper tube with kleenex. (2) Cover this solid bone, along with an unfilled one, with soil in a box. (3) Then unearth the bones. The hollow bone will be crushed. This happened to most of the small, hollow-boned dinosaurs' remains.

1   2   3

▲ You will need

The instructions in the Creative Corner box tell you what you need, including, plain and colored paper, cardboard, glue, string, rubber bands, scissors, pens or pencils, an eraser, modeling clay, crayons, paints, paintbrushes, markers, toilet paper tubes, drinking straws, plastic pots, tape, soil, wooden rods, twig, and plaster of paris.

▼ At the bottom of most of the right-hand pages in the book you will find one or two useful websites. These have been carefully chosen to add to the information on the page.

Early dinosaurs

Dinosaurs lived on Earth millions and millions of years ago. The age of dinosaurs began about 230 million years ago in a time we call the Triassic period. The first dinosaurs were small to medium-sized creatures. They were fast runners. Later in the Triassic, the plant-eating dinosaurs came along. They were by far the largest land animals of their time.

What are dinosaurs?

Dinosaurs were reptiles that lived on Earth long before humans existed. They first appeared about 230 million years ago during the Triassic period of Earth's history. They dominated life on land during the Jurassic and Cretaceous periods that followed next. But then they all died out.

▶ Young dinosaurs hatched from eggs, as most reptiles do today. Some dinosaurs even made nests and fed their young until they were big enough to leave the nest.

DINOSAUR LEGS

The legs of today's reptiles sprawl out to the sides, and the body sits beneath them, as with this Gila monster lizard. Dinosaurs had straight legs held underneath their bodies, similar to modern mammals.

Gila monster

Dinosaurs came in a variety of shapes and sizes. All of them lived on land. Some walked on two legs, and some walked on four. Some dinosaurs could do both.

There were plant-eating herbivores and meat-eating carnivores. Among them were lone hunters, pack hunters, such as these Coelophysis, scavengers, and herd animals.

WHAT MAKES A DINOSAUR?

All dinosaurs lived on land. They were reptiles with straight legs held underneath their bodies. Dinosaur experts can tell a dinosaur skeleton from details of its bones.

VOCABULARY

reptiles
Cold-blooded, scaly animals that usually reproduce by laying eggs.

scavengers
Animals that eat dead animals that they did not kill themselves.

INTERNET LINKS: www.nhm.ac.uk/kids-only/dinosaurs/

Fossils

We know that dinosaurs existed because they have left fossil remains in rocks that formed at the time. When the fossil of a dinosaur is found, a team of scientists, called paleontologists, get together. They excavate it, or dig it out of the ground. The fossil parts are then taken away to a laboratory to be examined.

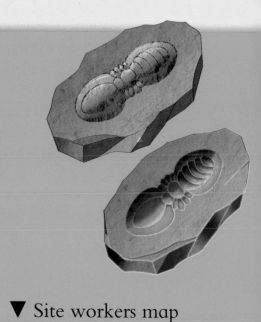

▼ Site workers map and photograph the fossils when they are in the ground. Once the fossils are removed, they are wrapped in plaster of Paris to protect them from breaking.

◀ If the hard parts of an animal buried in rock dissolve away, a hole called a mold may keep the original shape. Sometimes the mold fills with minerals that harden to form a fossil cast.

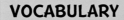

VOCABULARY

fossil
The remains of an animal or plant that died long ago, preserved in rock.

paleontologist
A scientist who studies fossils and ancient life, including dinosaurs.

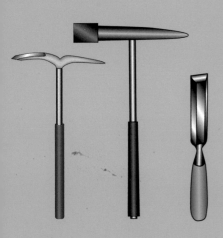

▲ When an animal dies, it may be covered in mud. Over millions of years, the mud becomes rock. The animal's hard parts turn to stone fossils. We can find the fossils when the rock wears away.

▲ Paleontologists use picks, hammers, and chisels to remove a fossil from the surrounding rock. In soft ground, they use a trowel instead. Brushes are used to sweep away soil gently from the bones.

Creative corner

Make a fossil of a twig

Press a twig into a piece of modeling clay. Then take it out. Mix some plaster of Paris and pour it into the twig shape. When the plaster is dry, remove the clay from your fossil twig.

INTERNET LINKS: www.sheppardsoftware.com/scienceforkids/dinosaurs/fossils_movie.htm

The Triassic scene

Before the Triassic period, life on Earth had existed for millions of years. But most of the animal species, or types, had become extinct, or died out, just before the Triassic. The beginning of the Triassic was a bleak time. The species that survived, and others that developed from them, filled the world again. Among them were the first dinosaurs.

▲ All of the land on Earth was joined together as one huge continent, known as Pangaea. The climate was generally hot and dry, but there was enough rainfall for many species of plants to survive.

THE PERMIAN EXTINCTION

As little as one-tenth of all animal species on Earth survived the mass extinction that came just before the beginning of the Triassic, called the Permian extinction. In the seas, trilobites (left), sea scorpions, and some coral groups were wiped out.

▶ The first dinosaurs lived alongside other groups of reptiles. Flying reptiles called pterosaurs soared in the skies. Other reptiles called aetosaurs (with armor), rhynchosaurs, and cynodonts lived on land. Crocodile-like reptiles called phytosaurs lived on land and in the water.

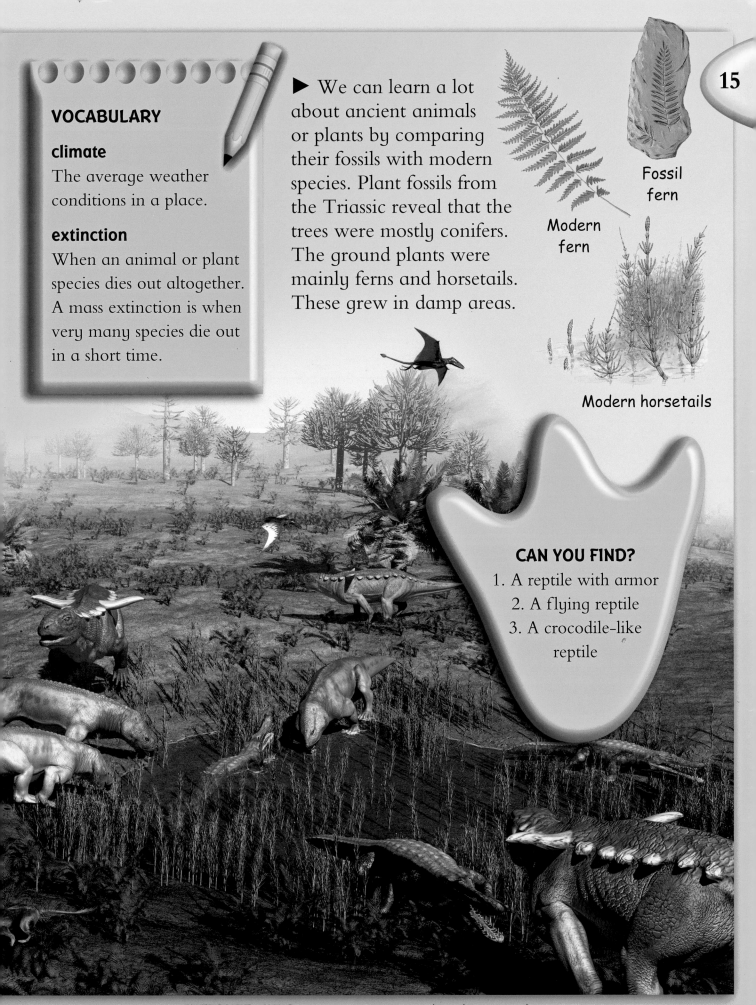

VOCABULARY

climate
The average weather conditions in a place.

extinction
When an animal or plant species dies out altogether. A mass extinction is when very many species die out in a short time.

► We can learn a lot about ancient animals or plants by comparing their fossils with modern species. Plant fossils from the Triassic reveal that the trees were mostly conifers. The ground plants were mainly ferns and horsetails. These grew in damp areas.

Fossil fern

Modern fern

Modern horsetails

CAN YOU FIND?
1. A reptile with armor
2. A flying reptile
3. A crocodile-like reptile

In the seas and skies

The reptiles that took over after the Permian extinction, in the early Jurassic period, adapted to live in many different surroundings. Some reptiles developed wings for gliding or flying through the skies. Many land reptiles went back to live in the sea. The reptiles of the seas and skies were not dinosaurs.

► Pterosaurs were flying reptiles. They appeared at the same time as the dinosaurs and existed throughout the age of dinosaurs. The earliest pterosaurs lived by the sea and hunted fish.

▼ Askeptosaurus was a long, eel-shaped creature that swam with S-shaped swings of its tail and narrow body. It steered through the water using its webbed feet.

WHY DO SOME ANIMALS GO BACK TO THE SEA?

The seas are full of fish and shellfish—all good food. Wherever there is something to eat, some animal will evolve to hunt and eat it.

GLIDING REPTILES

Some little reptiles, such as this Kuehneosaurus, had broad wings of skin stretched between long ribs of bone. They used these wings to glide from tree to tree, or from cliff top to cliff top.

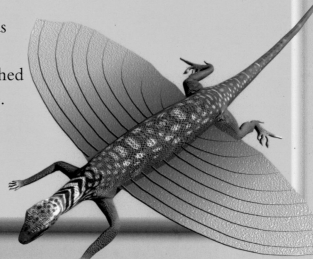

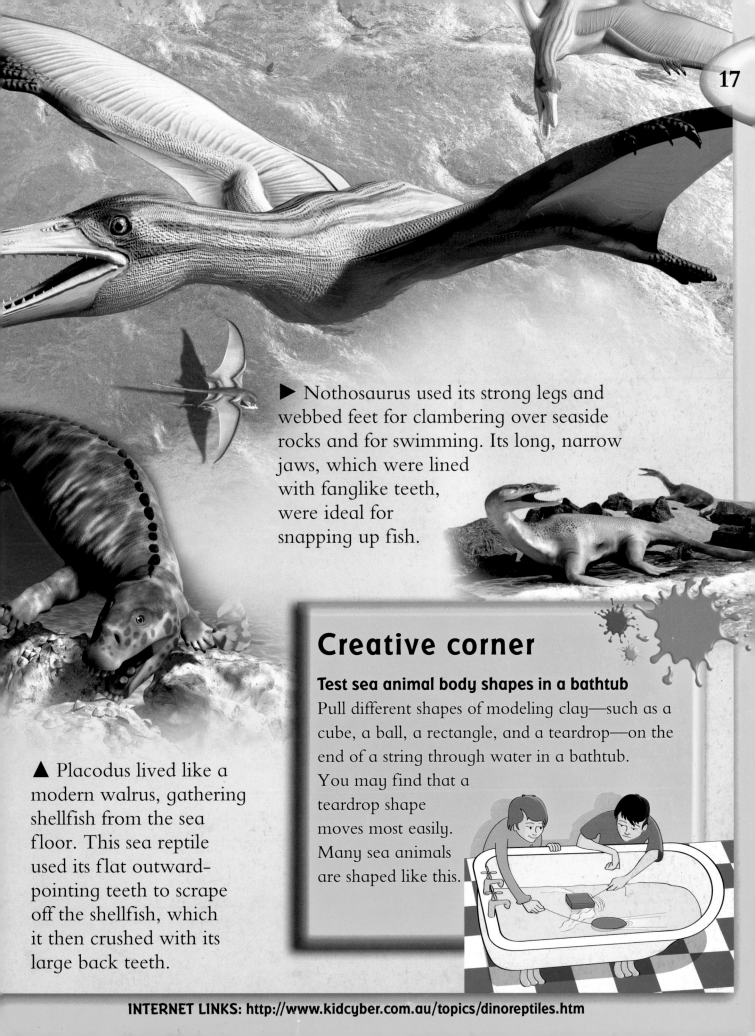

▶ Nothosaurus used its strong legs and webbed feet for clambering over seaside rocks and for swimming. Its long, narrow jaws, which were lined with fanglike teeth, were ideal for snapping up fish.

Creative corner

Test sea animal body shapes in a bathtub

Pull different shapes of modeling clay—such as a cube, a ball, a rectangle, and a teardrop—on the end of a string through water in a bathtub. You may find that a teardrop shape moves most easily. Many sea animals are shaped like this.

▲ Placodus lived like a modern walrus, gathering shellfish from the sea floor. This sea reptile used its flat outward-pointing teeth to scrape off the shellfish, which it then crushed with its large back teeth.

INTERNET LINKS: http://www.kidcyber.com.au/topics/dinoreptiles.htm

The first dinosaurs

The first dinosaurs appeared almost 230 million years ago. They belonged to a family of reptiles called the archosaurs. The earliest dinosaurs, such as Herrerasaurus and Eoraptor, were all bipedal hunters. When these creatures lived, dinosaurs were small and not very common.

Marasuchus skeleton

▲ Marasuchus and Herrerasaurus look very similar. But scientists can tell from details in the hip bones that Herrerasaurus was a true dinosaur, and Marasuchus was another type of archosaur.

VOCABULARY

bipedal
An animal that uses only two legs for walking.

salt gland
An organ in the skulls of some reptiles and birds that helps to remove salt from the blood.

▶ Eoraptor chased prey through low-growing forest plants in what is now Argentina in South America. This fox-sized dinosaur was probably a very fast runner because it had a light body and long, strong legs.

Marasuchus

Herrerasaurus
skeleton

Herrerasaurus

AMAZING!

Herrerasaurus and Eoraptor could stand almost upright and run on legs that were straight below their bodies. Most other reptiles in the Triassic had legs that sprawled out to the side.

▶ Like all other dinosaurs and their relatives, Herrerasaurus had a hole in its skull between the holes for its eyes and nostrils. This hole would have made the skull lighter. It would also have provided more room for muscles, and may have housed a salt gland.

CATCHING FOOD

The early dinosaurs probably fed on the small, lizardlike reptiles that were around at the time. The dinosaurs either snapped up their prey using their powerful jaws or grabbed it with their bony fingers.

INTERNET LINKS: www.dinosaurfact.net/Triassic/Eoraptor.php

Types of dinosaurs

Dinosaurs are divided into two main groups based on the shape of their hip bones. The groups are the saurischians and the ornithischians. A saurischian's hip bones were like those of a modern lizard. Ornithischians had hip bones that looked like those of a modern bird.

hip bones

▼ Paleontologists have figured out the family tree for all of the known dinosaur species. This tree shows us which types of dinosaurs were related to one another.

Tyrannosaurus

Diplodocus

THEROPODS

SAUROPODS

▲ The lizard-hipped dinosaurs, or saurischians, had three hip bones in a triangle shape. All of the carnivores, such as Staurikosaurus (above), and the long-necked herbivores were lizard-hipped.

VOCABULARY

family tree
A diagram showing ancestors and descendants.

stomach
A baglike structure in an animal's body. The stomach breaks down food that has been swallowed.

LIZARD-HIPPED
DINOSAURS

Marasuchus

NAMING DINOSAURS

The British scientist Sir Richard Owen gave dinosaurs their name in 1842. He created the word "dinosauria" from the Greek words for "terrible" and "lizard."

AMAZING!

Birds are descended from lizard-hipped dinosaurs, but they have hip bones like the bird-hipped dinosaurs!

Triceratops

Tenontosaurus

Stegosaurus

hip bones

MARGINOCEPHALIANS

ORNITHOPODS

THYREOPHORANS

BIRD-HIPPED DINOSAURS

WHY IS THE BIRD-HIPPED SHAPE USEFUL?

The bird-hipped skeleton leaves plenty of room for a large stomach. Plant eaters need a large stomach to handle the huge amounts of plant food they must eat.

▲ Bird-hipped dinosaurs, or ornithischians, had hip bones that were swept back. These dinosaurs were all plant eaters, such as Lesothosaurus (above) and all of the armored dinosaurs that came along later.

INTERNET LINKS: www.kids-dinosaurs.com/dinosaur-classification.html

Herd of hunters

Some early meat-eating dinosaurs hunted in packs, working together to take down animals larger than themselves. Scientists figure out which meat eaters lived in groups by examining fossil footprints and places called bone beds, which contain many dinosaurs that died at the same place at the same time.

WAS COELOPHYSIS A CANNIBAL?

One famous Coelophysis fossil was thought to have been a cannibal, with a baby Coelophysis in its stomach. But the "baby" turned out to be a young crocodile.

▼We know that Coelophysis hunted in packs like this one because more than 100 specimens were dug up at one site in New Mexico in 1947. Very few other animals were found during the excavations.

MAKING TRACKS

Sometimes when a dinosaur made a footprint in mud or sand, the print filled with more mud or sand. If the mud or sand turned to stone, the footprint could be preserved as a hollow mold, or as a solid cast.

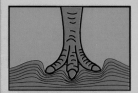
1. Print is made

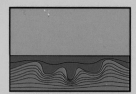
2. The print fills

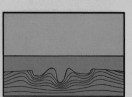
3. Stone forms

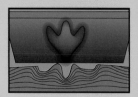
4. Fossils remain

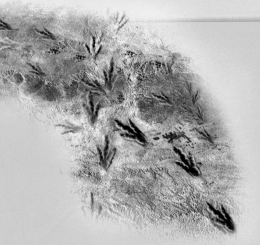

FOOTPRINT DEPTHS AND SHAPES

Dinosaurs left shallow footprints in firm soil. They left a deeper, more defined print in looser, damp soil. Wet mud collapsed in on itself as soon as the animal lifted out its foot.

| Faint dent | Shallow print | Semi-deep print | Deep print | Mud-collapsed |

▲When footprints of many of the same kind of dinosaur are found together, it shows that they probably lived in a group. These prints may have been made by a pack of Coelophysis stalking prey.

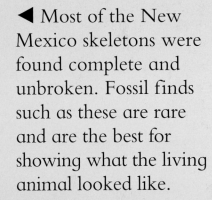

◄ Most of the New Mexico skeletons were found complete and unbroken. Fossil finds such as these are rare and are the best for showing what the living animal looked like.

▼Many paleontologists believe that the Coelophysis found in New Mexico died in a flood. It is thought that the floodwater swept away the animals and dumped them on a sandbar.

INTERNET LINKS: http://nmstatefossil.org

The first plant eaters

The earliest known plant-eating dinosaurs were long-necked creatures that appeared in the Late Triassic. They belonged to the same family as the meat eaters—the lizard-hipped dinosaurs. They were also the ancestors of the sauropods, the biggest land animals of all time.

▲ The Triassic plant eaters were bigger than the meat eaters. Their skeletons show that these creatures had heavy limbs to support their weight, as well as a long neck, which they could stretch upward.

LEAFLIKE TOOTH

Plateosaurus had small, leaf-shaped teeth with jagged edges. The teeth were not as sharp as a flesh-eating dinosaur's teeth, but they were good for stripping leaves from plants and trees.

HOW PLATEOSAURUS MOVED

Scientists use computer models such as this one to figure out how dinosaurs moved. The models show that Plateosaurus usually walked on its hind legs, but it could also walk on all four of its limbs.

▼ One of the smallest dinosaur skeletons known was that of a Mussaurus baby—so small that it would fit in your hands. The adult would have been about 10 ft. (3m) long—still much smaller than 26-ft. (8-m)-long Plateosaurus.

◀ Plateosaurus was one of the biggest plant-eating dinosaurs in the Triassic. Its large body was so heavy that it sometimes walked on all fours to support its weight. Plateosaurus stood on its hind legs to reach plant food in trees.

Creative corner

Make a chart of animal feeding habits

Watch the birds near your home—watch them feeding and look at what they eat. Some of them are carnivores and some are herbivores. Others are omnivores that live on a diet of both meat and plants. Make a chart of the three different types.

INTERNET LINKS: www.abc.net.au/dinosaurs/fact_files/dried/plateosaurus.htm

Famous Triassic sites

Paleontologists sometimes get lucky. They might discover a site like one in Bristol, England, where all sorts of animals were found preserved together. A herd of about 50 Plateosaurus was found at Trossingen, Germany. Sites such as these reveal a lot about dinosaur behavior.

▶ The Bristol fossil site gives us a picture of a harsh plateau, full of trenches and caves. Lizardlike animals and gliding reptiles lived alongside small, long-necked, plant-eating dinosaurs such as Thecodontosaurus.

VOCABULARY

plateau
An area of flat upland.

quicksand
Wet sand that sucks in and swallows up anything that stands on it.

WHAT OTHER ANIMALS HAVE BEEN FOUND IN THE CAVES?

Alongside Thecodontosaurus, there were spiky, lizardlike animals called Clevosaurus and gliding reptiles called Kuehneosaurus.

▼ We can imagine how the animals were preserved in the ancient caves. (1) A Thecodontosaurus grazes on vegetation growing near a cave entrance. (2) It falls in or is washed in by a flash flood. (3) It fossilizes in the mud that later fills the cave.

1. Feeding   2. Falling   3. Fossilizing

▼ There were several major excavations at Trossingen. In the 1920s, Friedrick von Huene directed teams of workers who dug away half a hillside. The rock was carried away in small trucks.

AMAZING!

Paleontologists puzzled for a long time about how the Trossingen herd might have died. Today, most paleontologists believe that the herd got stuck in quicksand and was attacked by meat eaters.

A changing world

The Triassic period ended about 200 million years ago with a mass extinction that wiped out about 75 percent of all animals. These included at least four major groups of large reptiles. No one knows why the extinction happened, but a change in climate might have been the cause.

▶ One of the major groups of reptiles that became extinct was a group of plant-eating armored reptiles—this Typothorax belonged to that group.

AMAZING!
Climate change can cause rainy regions to become dry—and dry regions to become rainy. Species can die out if they cannot cope with the new conditions.

▶Erupting volcanoes could have caused the extinction. The volcanoes would have put carbon dioxide and other gases into the atmosphere. The change in the makeup of the atmosphere could have caused a change in world climate conditions.

VOCABULARY

atmosphere
A blanket of gases almost 500 mi. (800km) thick that surrounds Earth.

carbon dioxide
One of the main gases in the atmosphere.

▼ Before they became extinct at the end of the Triassic, land-living, crocodile-like reptiles, such as Saurosuchus, were the dominant hunters. These beasts may have preyed on Rutiodon.

▼ Many crocodile-like reptiles that lived in water, such as Rutiodon, also died out at this time. It is clear from their sharp teeth and snapping jaws that these animals were hunters.

Creative corner

Make a volcano erupt

Build a volcano shape with modeling clay. Hollow out a hole in the center and put two tablespoons of baking soda inside. Pour some vinegar into the hole, and watch your volcano erupt!

▼ A group of mammal-like reptiles with tusks died out gradually over the course of the Late Triassic. These animals were distantly related to the mammals. They were also related to our own ancestors.

Dinosaurs take over

The mass extinction at the end of the Triassic cleared the way for the dinosaurs to take over. Instead of the extinct plant-eating armored reptiles, for example, there developed all sorts of plant-eating dinosaurs. Instead of the crocodile-like hunters, such as Rutiodon and Saurosuchus, there were meat-eating dinosaurs.

▲ Even some dinosaurs died out. Thecodontosaurus (above) became extinct, but new species of long-necked dinosaurs replaced it.

▶ The extinction line on this chart marks when the age of dinosaurs began. Survivors of this extinction also included reptiles of the air and the sea, along with snakes and lizards and crocodylomorphs.

VOCABULARY

ornithopod
Bird-hipped dinosaurs that were plant eaters.

theropod
A two-legged, meat-eating, lizard-hipped dinosaur with sharp teeth and claws.

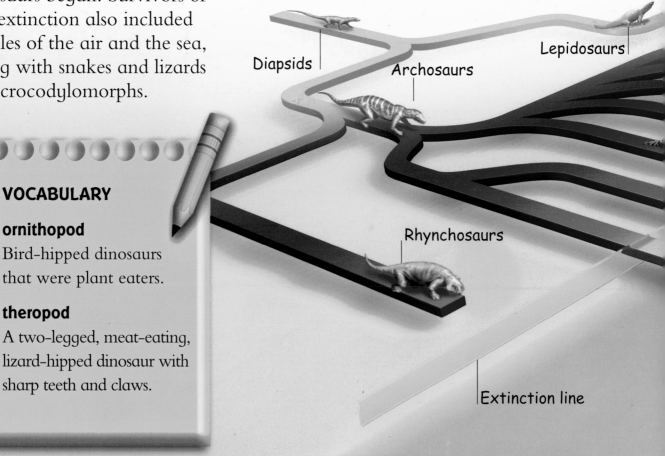

Diapsids

Archosaurs

Lepidosaurs

Rhynchosaurs

Extinction line

Other types of land animals disappeared, too, along with some plants. Many groups of shellfish and fish disappeared from the sea.

▶ Plant-eating ornithopods, including Fabrosaurus, began to grow in number. They probably had a way of life similar to that of the recently extinct armored reptiles.

◀ The type of hunting grounds once dominated by Saurosuchus were taken over by the meat-eating theropod dinosaurs such as Syntarsus.

Ichthyosaurs and plesiosaurs

Rauisuchians

Ornithosuchidae

Aetosaurs

Phytosaurs

Crocodylomorphs

Snakes and lizards

Pterosaurs

AMAZING!

Life on Earth nearly disappeared five times. The mass extinction at the end of the Triassic was the fourth one. The dinosaurs died out during the fifth one.

Dinosaurs

INTERNET LINKS: www.thebristoldinosaurproject.org.uk/?q=node/18

Now you know!

▲ Dinosaurs came in all shapes and sizes. There were meat eaters and plant eaters. They all lived on land between about 230 and 65 million years ago.

▲ Like most reptiles living today, dinosaurs laid eggs. Some mothers laid their eggs in nests and took care of their young.

▲ Fossils form in layers of sand and mud that eventually turn into solid rock. The fossils may be found when the rock wears away.

▶ Plant fossils from the Late Triassic show that there were mostly ferns (right) and conifers growing at the time.

▼ Pterosaurs were flying reptiles. They first appeared in the Late Triassic. They were not dinosaurs, but they were close relatives.

▲ Fossilized footprints give us clues about dinosaur life. They tell us whether the dinosaur was running or walking and whether it was in a group.

▲ Some dinosaurs had hip bones that were shaped like those of modern birds. The bird-hipped dinosaurs were all plant eaters.

▲ Some dinosaurs had hips that were shaped like those of modern lizards. Lizard-hipped dinosaurs included meat eaters and long-necked plant eaters.

A world of dinosaurs

The Jurassic period began about 205 million years ago. At the very beginning of the period, some dinosaurs were plant eaters and some lived by hunting. As time went by, their differences grew as groups began to develop special features of their own. Some had showy crests on their heads, and others had protective body armor. During the Early Jurassic, meat-eating dinosaurs began to get very big.

The Jurassic scene

The hot, dry climate of the Triassic gradually changed to a temperate climate during the Jurassic. New plants and animals suited to the new conditions developed, and old species began to flourish. The world became greener and fuller of animal life.

▶ The giant single continent, Pangaea, began to break up, and oceans spread into the gaps between the separated landmasses. Shallow seas spread over the new, low-lying coastal areas.

CAN YOU FIND?
1. A frog
2. A small furry animal
3. A crocodile
4. Horsetails

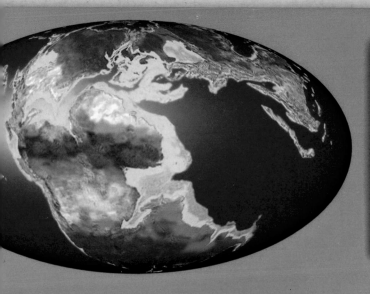

AMANG!

AMAZING!
Some deserts turned into swamps or tropical forests. Winds carried moisture to these regions from the shallow seas around the new coastal regions.

▶ The milder and moister climates of the Early and Middle Jurassic provided the ideal conditions for plants to grow. Forests of conifers and tree ferns, with an undergrowth of ferns and horsetails, began to spread to many parts of the world.

VOCABULARY

environment
The surroundings in which a plant or animal lives.

temperate
Mild weather, without extreme hot or cold temperatures.

▼ Crocodiles appeared in the Late Triassic, and in the Early Jurassic, some became sea dwellers. However, Protosuchus lived on land. It probably competed with the dinosaurs for the same food, such as fish and small land animals.

◀ Fossils from a Middle Jurassic site in central England show some of the animals that lived at the time. As well as dinosaurs, there were pterosaurs, crocodiles, small furry animals, and the earliest mammals and frogs.

Bird feet

A group of bird-hipped herbivores, called ornithopods, appeared in the Early Jurassic. They were given the name ornithopod, or "bird foot," because their feet looked like modern birds' feet. The first ornithopods were small, two-legged animals. Later ones were bigger, and some walked on all fours.

▼ Lesothosaurus was an Early Jurassic ornithopod. Its long legs, short arms, lightweight body, and slender tail all suggest that it was a fast, agile runner.

AMAZING!

Two Lesothosaurus were found curled up together in southern Africa. They died while they were sleeping underground to avoid the summer heat.

VOCABULARY

herbivores
Animals that eat only plants.

plains
Areas of flat land with very few tall trees.

▶ Lesothosaurus (above) lived in small groups on the hot plains of what is now southern Africa. Other ornithopods, such as Heterodontosaurus, lived there as well. The dinosaurs could live together because they probably fed on different types of plants.

▼ The only fossils belonging to Alocodon are its teeth. They look like ornithopod teeth, so scientists believe that Alocodon was an ornithopod. It lived during the Middle Jurassic in what is now Portugal.

▼ Like the other early ornithopods, Xiaosaurus was bipedal and had four toes on its birdlike feet. This Middle Jurassic ornithopod is known from just a few fossil bone fragments that were found in China.

WHAT OTHER BIRD FEATURES DID ORNITHOPODS HAVE?
As well as birdlike feet and hips, all ornithopods had beaks. These were ideal for snipping plants to eat.

INTERNET LINKS: www.bbc.co.uk/nature/life/Ornithopod

Browsers and grazers

38

Early Jurassic plant eaters were suited to feeding on the plants that grew at the time. Some dinosaurs browsed, or fed on the leaves and shoots of the high branches, while others grazed, or fed on the low plants of the undergrowth.

AMAZING!
Lufengosaurus herds left trails of destruction behind them as they roamed southwest China in the Early Jurassic. The animals stripped an area of all its plant life before they moved on to new feeding grounds.

▼ Lufengosaurus was built for browsing. It could reach high branches if it reared up and stretched its neck. This dinosaur may also have used a claw on its thumb to rake leaves from the trees.

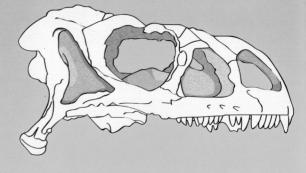

▲ Small, sharp teeth lined Lufengosaurus's jaws. Some scientists think that the teeth were suited to the diet of an omnivore. But others say the teeth are similar to those of modern iguanas, which are plant-eating lizards.

◀ Grazing ornithopods, such as Heterodontosaurus, had pouches in their cheeks. The pouches held on to food while it was being ground up by the back teeth.

WHAT WERE THE FANGS FOR?

Heterodontosaurus may have used its fangs to root for food in the ground. But it is more likely that the teeth were used in mating displays and for defense.

VOCABULARY

incisor
A narrow-edged tooth at the front of the mouth. It is used for cutting food.

mating display
A ritual performed to attract a mate during the breeding season.

▼ Heterodontosaurus had a beak in the front of its mouth to snip off leaves and shoots. It had sharp, pointed incisors as well, to help in gathering food. Its back teeth were flat and ground up the dinosaur's food. It had fangs, too, which may have been for feeding or for showing off!

Treetop feeder

Massospondylus was a successful treetop feeder that could survive in many different parts of the Early Jurassic world. Its fossil remains have been found in North America, Asia, and Africa. This proves that Massospondylus was able to feed on the various trees that grew in the different regions.

monkey-puzzle twig

gastroliths

TOUGH DIET
Massospondylus could eat tough coniferous plants, like modern monkey-puzzle trees, even though it could not chew. Instead, the dinosaur swallowed stones, known as gastroliths, which ground up the plants in its stomach.

▶ Scientists once thought that Massospondylus walked on all fours and raised itself up onto its hind legs to feed in trees. It is now believed that the dinosaur was bipedal but dropped down onto its hands to eat ground plants.

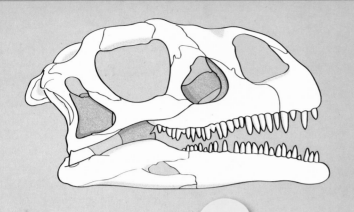

◀ Massospondylus had a small head relative to its body size. Its jaws were lined with peglike teeth. The shape of the teeth was ideal for stripping twigs and leaves from trees but not for chewing them.

DO ANY MODERN ANIMALS SWALLOW STONES?

Modern plant-eating birds, such as turkeys and pheasants, swallow pieces of grit to help grind up their food. They have beaks instead of teeth so they cannot chew.

AMAZING!

Smoothed gastroliths have been found in Massospondylus skeletons. It is thought that when the gastroliths had been worn smooth, the dinosaur would regurgitate them.

▼ Massospondylus could use its hands to support its weight when it was on all fours. This dinosaur may also have used its hands to grasp plants and then strip them using its thumb claws.

thumb claw

INTERNET LINKS: www.dinosaurfact.net/jurassic/Massospondylus.php

Long-necked dinosaurs

A group of large, long-necked, four-legged dinosaurs called sauropods appeared in the Middle Jurassic. Cetiosaurus, the biggest of the early sauropods, was the length of a sperm whale. Sauropods from the Late Jurassic were more than twice that size.

WHAT DOES CETIOSAURUS MEAN?

The name means "whale lizard." The dinosaur was given the name by Richard Owen in 1841. He knew that this giant was a reptile but thought that it swam in the sea.

▲ Shunosaurus, from Middle Jurassic China, was about 33 ft. (10m) long from its snout to the tip of its tail. It was short-necked for a sauropod, so it probably browsed ground plants rather than tall trees.

▲ Sauropods lived and traveled in herds. Trackways show that the young traveled in the middle of the herd, with the adults on the outside for protection.

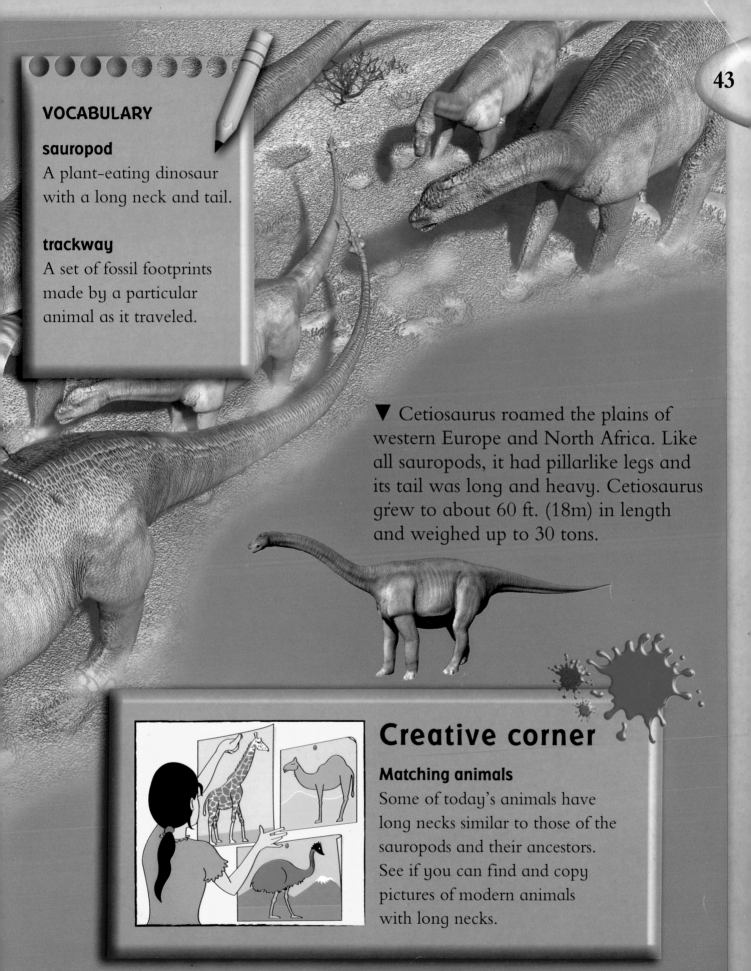

VOCABULARY

sauropod
A plant-eating dinosaur with a long neck and tail.

trackway
A set of fossil footprints made by a particular animal as it traveled.

▼ Cetiosaurus roamed the plains of western Europe and North Africa. Like all sauropods, it had pillarlike legs and its tail was long and heavy. Cetiosaurus grew to about 60 ft. (18m) in length and weighed up to 30 tons.

Creative corner

Matching animals
Some of today's animals have long necks similar to those of the sauropods and their ancestors. See if you can find and copy pictures of modern animals with long necks.

Armored dinosaurs

In the Early Jurassic, some plant-eating dinosaurs began to develop body armor for protection against predators. Early armored dinosaurs, such as Scelidosaurus and Scutellosaurus, had rows of bony plates and studs, called scutes, on their skin. The armor of later armored dinosaurs was even more advanced and threatening.

▼ We know from fossil finds that Scelidosaurus grazed on the shores of southern England. It had short legs, so it could not outrun many predators. But its body armor could bring a theropod's bite to a crunching full stop.

▼ Scelidosaurus's skin (below) was covered in pea-sized scales and rows of scutes. These added protection to the dinosaur's neck, back, and sides. But the armor was not perfect, as a predator could nip at the unarmored parts.

AMANZING!

In 1863, Richard Owen described the first Scelidosaurus skeleton ever found while it was still encased in rock. This rock was not removed from the fossil until the 1960s.

▲ Scutellosaurus had more than 300 scutes on its back, sides, and tail. It walked on two legs, but its armor made its body heavy in the front, so it probably walked on all fours as well.

MODERN ARMORED ANIMAL

A modern armadillo has armor to protect it from the claws and jaws of meat eaters. It is almost impossible for a predator to get through to an armadillo's soft body when the animal rolls itself into a tight ball. The early armored dinosaurs were not as well protected.

The first stegosaurs

Stegosaurs were a group of four-legged, plant-eating dinosaurs with impressive body armor. Early stegosaurs included Huayangosaurus and Dacentrurus. These creatures had rows of tall bony plates jutting up from their necks, backs, and tails, and their bulky bodies carried relatively small heads.

VOCABULARY

stegosaurs
A group of four-legged, bird-hipped dinosaurs from the Jurassic and Early Cretaceous periods.

walnut
A wrinkly nut that you can eat.

▲ Huayangosaurus's armor protected its back from the jaws of meat eaters. It also helped make the dinosaur look big and fierce, so a predator would think twice about attacking it. Spikes on the end of the tail made it a useful weapon of defense.

Tail spikes for defense

AMAZING!
Stegosaurs had brains the size of a walnut. This is tiny when compared with their overall size. It is possible that these creatures were not very bright.

WERE THE PLATES ONLY FOR DEFENSE?

The plates may have helped stegosaurs of the same species recognize one another. They may also have absorbed heat from the Sun to keep the dinosaur warm.

▼ The skeleton of the Late Jurassic stegosaur Dacentrurus is known only from a handful of bones. They are shown in this illustration (below left). But we can figure out what the whole skeleton and the animal looked like (below) by comparing it with the skeletons of better-known stegosaurs.

INTERNET LINKS: http://animals.howstuffworks.com/dinosaurs/dacentrurus.htm

Getting bigger

Fossil footprints and bones from the Early Jurassic show that meat-eating dinosaurs got much bigger at this time. One of the first of the large meat eaters was Dilophosaurus, a striking creature with two head crests. This hunter probably preyed on large plant eaters.

AMAZING!

Dilophosaurus's most unusual feature was its head crests, but some Dilophosaurus have been found without them. It is possible that only the male dinosaurs had crests.

▼ Dilophosaurus was about 20 ft. (6m) long from its snout to its tail and about 5 ft. (1.5m) tall at the hips. This Early Jurassic theropod was more than twice the size of Coelophysis, one of the biggest meat eaters in the Triassic.

Killer claws

There were sharp, curved claws on each of the three fingers on Dilophosaurus's hand. When it attacked, the dinosaur probably used the claws to slash and tear at its prey until the prey fell to the ground.

human
adult

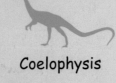
Coelophysis

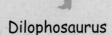
Dilophosaurus

◀ Footprints were found beside two Dilophosaurus skeletons in Arizona. They are 12 in. (30cm) long. In this illustration, you can see how much bigger the Arizona prints are compared with typical Coelophysis footprints.

▶ The bony head crests were probably used in mating displays. They would have made the male look bigger than he actually was. This might have attracted a female and scared off smaller rivals.

Creative corner

Make Dilophosaurus head crests

(1) Fold a piece of cardboard in half and cut out crest shapes like the ones here. (2) Paint one side of each of the crests. (3) Tape them together when the paint is dry. (4) Look in the mirror to see how much larger your head looks when you wear the crests.

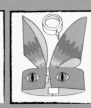

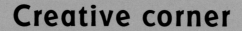

1 2 3 4

Antarctic dinosaurs

Today, the continent of Antarctica sits over the South Pole. The Antarctic climate is so cold that the only people who stay there are scientists, and no reptiles live there. Antarctica lay farther north in the Early Jurassic, so it was warmer and there was no permanent ice then. Dinosaurs could live there.

WHERE DID THE DINOSAURS GO IN THE WINTER?
In the Early Jurassic, Antarctica and Africa were connected to each other. The dinosaurs may have traveled north to Africa to escape the cold winters.

▲ Cryolophosaurus was the first Antarctic dinosaur to be named. The spectacular bony crest on this flesh-eating theropod's forehead may have been brightly colored and used for signaling to others.

▶ Paleontologists have found only leg and foot bones for this Antarctic dinosaur, called Glacialisaurus. The fossil remains show that this long-necked plant eater is related to Lufengosaurus, a dinosaur from China.

AMAZING!

The Antarctic fossil finds include pterosaur bone fragments and parts of some other, unidentified dinosaurs. Tree trunks have also been found.

▼ Digging for dinosaurs in Antarctica is difficult. Paleontologists can work only during the short summer season, when it is light and some of the snow melts. Special power tools must be used to cut into the frozen ground, and helicopters are needed to get to and from the site.

Stiff tails

Most of the medium- to large-sized theropods were tetanurans. The name means "stiff tails" and the dinosaurs are called this because they held out their tails stiffly to balance them as they moved on two legs. The first known stiff-tailed dinosaurs include Megalosaurus and Eustreptospondylus, which were large bipedal carnivores from Middle Jurassic southern England.

HOW CAN YOU TELL A STIFF-TAILED DINOSAUR FROM OTHER THEROPODS?
A stiff-tailed dinosaur has an extra hole in its skull in front of its eyes, and its teeth are positioned toward the front of its mouth.

VOCABULARY

balance
To keep something steady so that it does not fall.

carnivores
Animals that eat other animals, or meat.

torso
An animal's body from the neck to the hips.

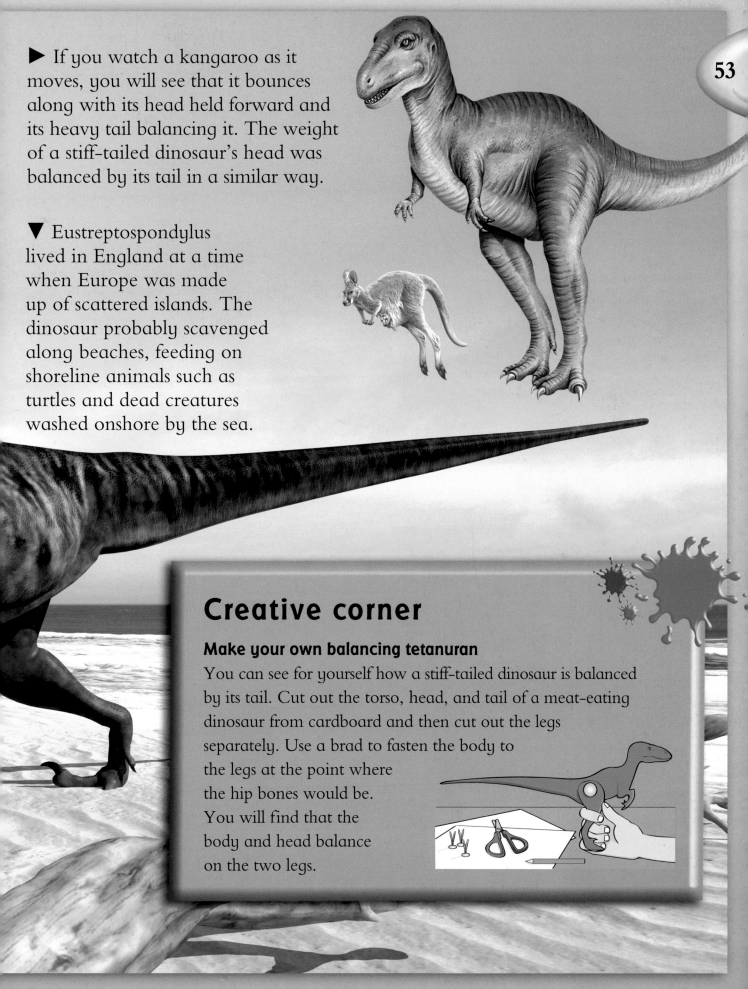

► If you watch a kangaroo as it moves, you will see that it bounces along with its head held forward and its heavy tail balancing it. The weight of a stiff-tailed dinosaur's head was balanced by its tail in a similar way.

▼ Eustreptospondylus lived in England at a time when Europe was made up of scattered islands. The dinosaur probably scavenged along beaches, feeding on shoreline animals such as turtles and dead creatures washed onshore by the sea.

Creative corner

Make your own balancing tetanuran

You can see for yourself how a stiff-tailed dinosaur is balanced by its tail. Cut out the torso, head, and tail of a meat-eating dinosaur from cardboard and then cut out the legs separately. Use a brad to fasten the body to the legs at the point where the hip bones would be. You will find that the body and head balance on the two legs.

Terror of the Jurassic

A giant theropod called Megalosaurus dominated all other land animals in Jurassic England, France, and Portugal. This hunter was the first dinosaur ever to be named. The British geologist William Buckland named and described it in 1824, based on a piece of jaw and a small collection of bones.

VOCABULARY

geologist
A scientist who studies rocks, fossils, and the history of Earth.

vertebrae
The bones that make up an animal's backbone, or spine.

▶ Megalosaurus was a bulky, 30 ft. (9m) hunter that ate any animal it could catch in its lethal claws. It could run fast, so this young stegosaur (right) is easy prey and will soon be in the predator's powerful jaws.

◀ For centuries, quarry workers had uncovered fossil Megalosaurus parts in the limestone quarries of Oxfordshire, England. But scientists began to study these remains only in the early 1800s.

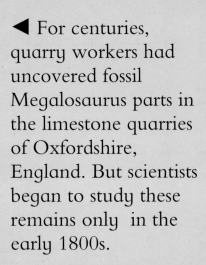

NAMING THE BIG LIZARD
Buckland studied fragments of pelvis, some vertebrae, limbs, and a jaw and decided that they belonged to a huge lizard. He called the animal Megalosaurus, which is Greek for "great lizard."

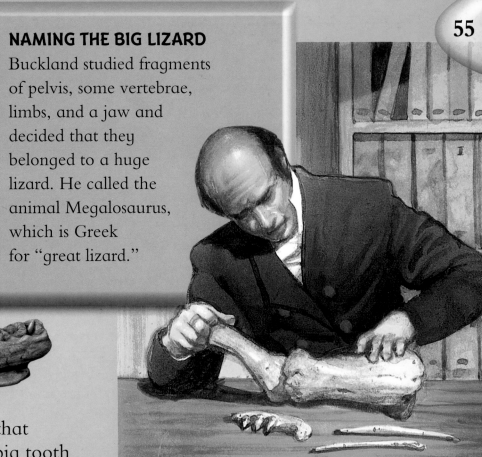

▲ The Megalosaurus jaw that Buckland studied had one big tooth and several new, growing teeth. These may have been replacing teeth lost when the dinosaur bit its victims.

Creative corner

Make a moving Megalosaurus jaw
Cut triangular teeth shapes along two strips of cardboard. Now punch holes at both ends of the two strips. Line up the holes and then push a pencil through them, bending the cardboard into a curved shape. Wind rubber bands around the ends of the pencil to keep the jaws in place.

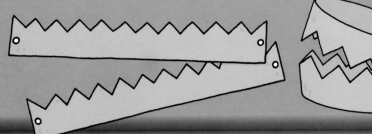

INTERNET LINKS: www.oum.ox.ac.uk/learning/pdfs/buckland.pdf

Up in the air

The Jurassic skies were filled with flying insects and pterosaurs. Most of the pterosaurs had teeth, long tails, and short necks and wrists. One of these pterosaurs, Dimorphodon, came from Early Jurassic southern England. Its large head and beak resembled those of a modern-day puffin. This flying reptile had a long tail with a diamond-shaped flap of skin on the end of it.

MARY ANNING

Several skeletons of Dimorphodon have been unearthed. The first one was found in 1828 by the fossil hunter Mary Anning. She made her name in the early 1800s finding and selling skeletons near her home in Lyme Regis on the coast of southern England. They were the skeletons of Jurassic sea animals.

▶ Dimorphodon flew well using its light yet large wings, which extended out about 5 ft. (1.5m). Its long, thin tail helped to keep it balanced as it flew. This pterosaur probably fed on fish, small vertebrates (animals with a backbone) and insects, snapping them up and holding them in its wide, toothed jaws.

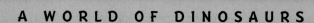

?

WHY DO ANIMALS FLY?

Several groups of animals have taken to the skies throughout animal history. They may have done this to escape predators on the land or to hunt flying prey such as insects.

AMAZING!

Scientists are sure that there were types of pterosaurs that lived inland, but no one has found their fossils. Most of the known pterosaurs are believed to have lived beside water because their skeletons were found in rocks formed from sea or lake sediments.

INTERNET LINKS: www.ucmp.berkeley.edu/history/anning.html

Below the waves

No dinosaurs lived under the sea, but other types of reptiles lived there in the Early and Middle Jurassic. Among them were crocodiles and ichthyosaurs. There were also long-necked and short-necked plesiosaurs swimming around.

▼ Ichthyosaurs, such as Ophthalmosaurus (below), moved through the water by beating their tails from side to side. The plesiosaurs zoomed through the water by flapping their four flippers.

AMAZING!

Shastasaurus, the largest ichthyosaur found so far, was about 75 ft.(23m) long. The head alone was longer than a killer whale. Its fossil was discovered in British Columbia, Canada, in 1991.

ICHTHYOSAUR SKELETON

This ichthyosaur fossil shows that these reptiles had streamlined, teardrop-shaped bodies that could glide through the water with ease. Their small snouts suggest that they ate only small prey, including fish, squid, and other marine animals.

▲ Liopleurodon was one of the biggest marine predators of Jurassic times. Its sharp-toothed jaws were up to 5 ft. (1.5m) long, so giant fish, ichthyosaurs, and marine crocodiles were easy prey for this beast.

▼ Metriorhynchus used its long, powerful tail in a sideways-sweeping motion to move its streamlined body through the water. This marine crocodile lived in shallow seas, hunting everything from slow-moving ammonites to faster-moving fish.

INTERNET LINKS: www.bbc.co.uk/nature/life/Ichthyosaur

Jurassic food web

A food web shows who ate what in a certain place. In the Jurassic period, some dinosaurs ate plants. These plant-eating dinosaurs were eaten by theropods. Smaller, insect-eating animals in the Jurassic food web were eaten by small predators, such as crocodiles, or even by theropods.

▶ Theropod dinosaurs, such as Megalosaurus, were at the top of the Jurassic food web. They ate plant-eating dinosaurs and any other animal they could catch.

FOOD WEBS IN JURASSIC SEAS

The Jurassic seas were full of life. Each creature had its own place in a food web. Sea webs start with microscopic plants, called phytoplankton. In Jurassic times, little fish ate the phytoplankton and ammonites ate the fish. The ammonites were eaten by ichthyosaurs, which in turn were eaten by the mighty pliosaurs.

▲ Plant-eating dinosaurs, such as the sauropod Cetiosaurus, got the energy they needed to move and grow by eating plants.

Megalosaurus

**WHO EATS
THE PREDATORS AT
THE TOP OF THE WEB?**
Few of the smaller Jurassic
meat eaters would have dared to
take on the large theropods. But
when the top predators died,
smaller animals fed on
their remains.

Cetiosaurus

Kuehneotherium

► Kuehneotherium was a
type of Jurassic mammal.
Like modern shrews, it
hunted and ate insects.
Juralibellula may have
been one of its victims.

▼ All food webs start with
plants. They can make
their own food from water
and carbon dioxide using
light energy from the Sun.

Juralibellula

▲ Insects nibbled
the fern leaves
and sucked the
sap. Larger, meat-
eating insects, such as
prehistoric dragonflies,
ate the small insects.

Ferns

INTERNET LINKS: www.bbc.co.uk/nature/history_of_the_earth/Jurassic

Re-creating the past

It is because of the scientists who study and piece together dinosaur fossils that we can enjoy discovering these amazing animals. Dinosaur exhibits draw lines of visitors to museums, and dinosaur theme parks are just as popular. There are also countless books, movies, and cartoons about them.

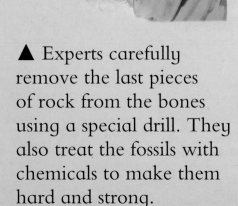

▲ Experts carefully remove the last pieces of rock from the bones using a special drill. They also treat the fossils with chemicals to make them hard and strong.

ARE MUSEUM RECONSTRUCTIONS REAL FOSSILS?

Usually scientists make copies of the bones in a tough material, such as plastic, and put these copies on display. The original fossils are kept for the scientists to study.

◄ It takes years to build a dinosaur skeleton for exhibition in a museum. Usually it is made up of copies of bones of more than one individual. Missing bones are created from scratch.

◄ To get a good picture of what a dinosaur's life was like, paleontologists study fossils of the plants and other animals living at the time.

JURASSIC PARK

Dinosaur movies and cartoons often get the facts wrong. In the movie "Jurassic Park," for example, Dilophosaurus had a neck frill and was able to spit poison. Neither of these things was true in real life.

▼ The world's first dinosaur theme park was attracting crowds to Crystal Palace in England only 12 years after Richard Owen invented the word "dinosauria." The theme park opened in 1854, and had sculptures of Jurassic dinosaurs that were designed by Owen.

VOCABULARY

exhibits
Objects that are displayed in public—for example, in a museum.

reconstruction
A dinosaur skeleton that is built up piece by piece from the bones.

INTERNET LINKS: www.sciencekids.co.nz/sciencefacts/earth/fossils.html

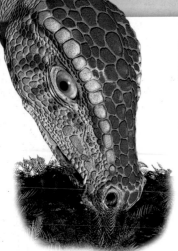

Now you know!

▲ Most plant-eating dinosaurs had cheek pouches. The animals probably stored food in the pouches while they fed.

▲ Some dinosaurs swallowed stomach stones to help them digest their food.

▲ The early stegosaurs had armor made of bony plates and spikes.

▲ Dilophosaurus may have used the crests on its head to attract mates and scare off rivals.

▲ Many of the larger theropods had stiff and heavy tails. These gave the dinosaurs balance as they moved along on two legs.

▲ Ichthyosaurs were dolphinlike reptiles that moved through the water by beating their tail from side to side.

◀ Mary Anning disovered the fossil bones of many Jurassic sea reptiles, as well as the pterosaur Dimorphodon, in England in the early 1800s.

◀ Scientists study plant fossils, footprints, and the fossils of other animals to build up a picture of what a dinosaur's life was like.

Giant dinosaurs

The Late Jurassic, which began about 167 million years ago, was the time of giant dinosaurs. The largest of these were the massive, long-necked, plant-eating sauropods. Herds of them dominated the landscape, which was also filled with big armored dinosaurs. The plant eaters fell prey to large and small meat-eating dinosaurs. These meat eaters were armed with powerful jaws, and lethal claws and teeth. Huge reptiles were also to be found in the sea and the air during the Late Jurassic.

The Late Jurassic scene

The Late Jurassic climate was warm and moist, allowing lush tropical vegetation to grow over vast areas. Dinosaurs became larger and more varied. Pterosaurs still ruled the skies, but the first bird, Archaeopteryx, developed and took to the air at this time.

▲ Pangaea was split into two supercontinents—Laurasia in the north and Gondwana in the south. The Atlantic Ocean started to separate Eurasia and North America. A shallow sea flooded central Europe and separated it from Asia.

VOCABULARY

lagoon
A body of salt water separated from the sea by sandbars, reefs, or islands.

tropical
Hot and humid weather. Tropical plants need these conditions to grow.

CAN YOU FIND?
1. A sauropod browsing
2. A sauropod grazing

▲ Fossils that formed in a lagoon in what is now part of southern Germany show some of the animals that were living there at the time. There were small dinosaurs, pterosaurs (right), and the first bird, Archaeopteryx (above).

◄ By the Late Jurassic, dinosaurs lived in almost every part of the world. The sauropods increased in number. They roamed the landscape in large herds that ate up huge areas of plants.

Creative corner

Make a Jurassic landscape

Create the land and sea with modeling clay and cardboard. Cut lines around rolled up paper, as shown, to make the leaves and trunks of the plants. You could cover the trunks with modeling clay to attach them to the land.

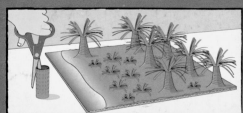

INTERNET LINKS: http://animals.howstuffworks.com/dinosaurs/middle-and-late-jurassic-periods.htm

Early bird

One of the most important fossils ever found was of Archaeopteryx, in Germany in 1860. The fossil is about 150 million years old and shows a creature that looks part dinosaur and part bird. This probably proves that birds developed from a type of dinosaur. Archaeopteryx could fly, but not very far and not very well.

WHICH BIRD FEATURES DID ARCHAEOPTERYX HAVE?
Like modern birds, Archaeopteryx had flying feathers (arranged like a bird's), a lightweight body with mostly hollow bones, and a wishbone.

HAND EVOLUTION

Enough fossil hands exist to show how theropods developed into birds. (1) Early theropods had four or five fingers on each hand. (2) Later theropods had two or three fingers. (3) Later still, advanced theropods had long fingers with large claws. (4) Archaeopteryx had slim fingers. (5) Modern birds have thin fingers and no claws. The three fingers are fused, or stuck, together so that they support the weight of the bird's wings.

1. Heterodontosaurus

2. Allosaurus

3. Ornitholestes

4. Archaeopteryx

5. Modern chicken

▶ The claws on Archaeopteryx's toes and fingers were ideal for climbing up tree trunks, so it is likely that this creature lived in trees. It is also likely that it could fly from tree to tree, but it was probably unable to stay in the air for long.

▶ Ten Archaeopteryx fossils have been found in Solnhofen, Germany. They formed in fine-grained limestone, which not only shows the bones but also the impression of the tail and wing feathers.

LOST FEATURES

A typical modern bird has lost some of the features that Archaeopteryx had. It does not have hand claws, teeth, a flat breastbone, belly ribs, or a long, bony tail. These would make the bird too heavy to fly.

VOCABULARY

evolution
A process in which living things change gradually over millions of years.

limestone
Rock formed from shells and other animal remains.

Hollow bones

There are few fossil remains of small, Late Jurassic theropods. This is because they had hollow bones that were very fragile and crushed easily. Among the small theropods that we know about are Compsognathus and Ornitholestes. These dinosaurs are close relatives of modern birds.

WERE ALL HOLLOW-BONED THEROPODS SMALL?

The hollow-boned theropods of the Late Jurassic eventually developed into the huge tyrannosaurs. These were the top predators of the Late Cretaceous.

VOCABULARY

jackals
Wild dogs from Asia and Africa. They are closely related to wolves.

tyrannosaurs
A group of very large theropods that lived in the Cretaceous period.

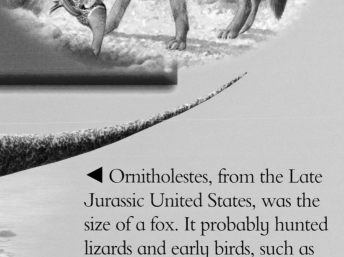

MODERN SCAVENGERS

Small and medium-sized theropods probably lived like modern foxes and jackals. These hunt for small mammals, birds, and reptiles but also eat dead animals when they find them.

◀ Ornitholestes, from the Late Jurassic United States, was the size of a fox. It probably hunted lizards and early birds, such as Archaeopteryx, but it may also have tackled larger prey than little Compsognathus did.

◀ Compsognathus was the size of a chicken. It hunted and scavenged on the coasts of warm islands in what are now southern Germany and France. This creature's slim build and birdlike legs would have made it a fast mover.

Creative corner

Hollow and solid bone test

(1) Make a solid "bone" by packing a toilet paper tube with kleenex. (2) Cover this solid bone, along with an unfilled one, with soil in a box. (3) Then unearth the bones. The hollow bone will be crushed. This happened to most of the small, hollow-boned dinosaurs' remains.

1

2

3

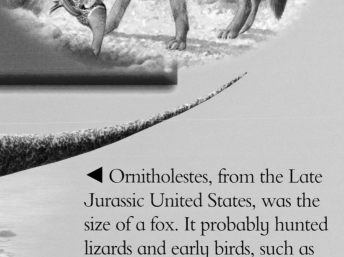

71

Big meat eaters

Theropods got bigger and bigger as the Jurassic period went on. Their jaws became longer, and their teeth grew in size. Their legs became more powerful, giving them the speed and strength to hunt down and kill even larger prey than they did before.

AMAZING!

Elaphrosaurus was about the same weight as a modern lion, yet it was about three times the size of a lion. Scientists believe that Elaphrosaurus's slender build was designed for speed and that it was an extremely fast runner.

VOCABULARY

formation
An area of rocks, or layers of rocks, that share the same features.

nimble
If an animal is nimble, it is light on its feet and can move and act quickly.

◀ Lourinhanosaurus, from Late Jurassic Portugal, probably ate large animals such as stegosaurs. Stomach stones have been found in this predator's fossil remains. The stones helped the dinosaur digest its food.

▼ Elaphrosaurus was more than 20 ft. (6m) long and 5 ft. (1.5m) tall at the hips. It was a nimble hunter that may have preyed on smaller dinosaurs, as well as lizards and mammals.

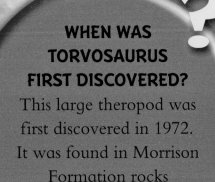

? WHEN WAS TORVOSAURUS FIRST DISCOVERED?

This large theropod was first discovered in 1972. It was found in Morrison Formation rocks in Colorado.

▲ Torvosaurus was one of the largest meat eaters living in Late Jurassic North America. It was about 33 ft. (10m) long and 8 ft. (2.5m) tall at the hips. This predator was big and fierce enough to kill medium-sized sauropods.

▶ Yangchuanosaurus, from Late Jurassic China, was more than 36 ft. (11m) long. It was able to kill large sauropods. Its massive tail was almost half its total length, and its skull was up to 3.6 ft. (1.1m) long.

Jurassic hunter

Allosaurus was a ferocious predator that roamed North America, East Africa, and southwest Europe in Late Jurassic times. This theropod could grow to about 33 ft. (10m) in length. It was powerful enough to attack prey much larger than itself, such as the 75-ft. (23-m)-long sauropod Apatosaurus.

AMING!

Over 40 Allosaurus, found in a quarry in Utah, died when they got trapped in mud. They were trying to get to plant-eating dinosaurs already stuck there.

DID ALLOSAURUS HUNT IN GROUPS?

It is possible that Allosaurus hunted in packs. This would explain why the fossil remains of several individuals have been found together at different sites.

▶ A pack of scavenging Ceratosaurus descend on a sauropod that was brought down by an Allosaurus. The attacker weakened its victim by hacking at it with its top jaw, using its feet to stop the prey from struggling.

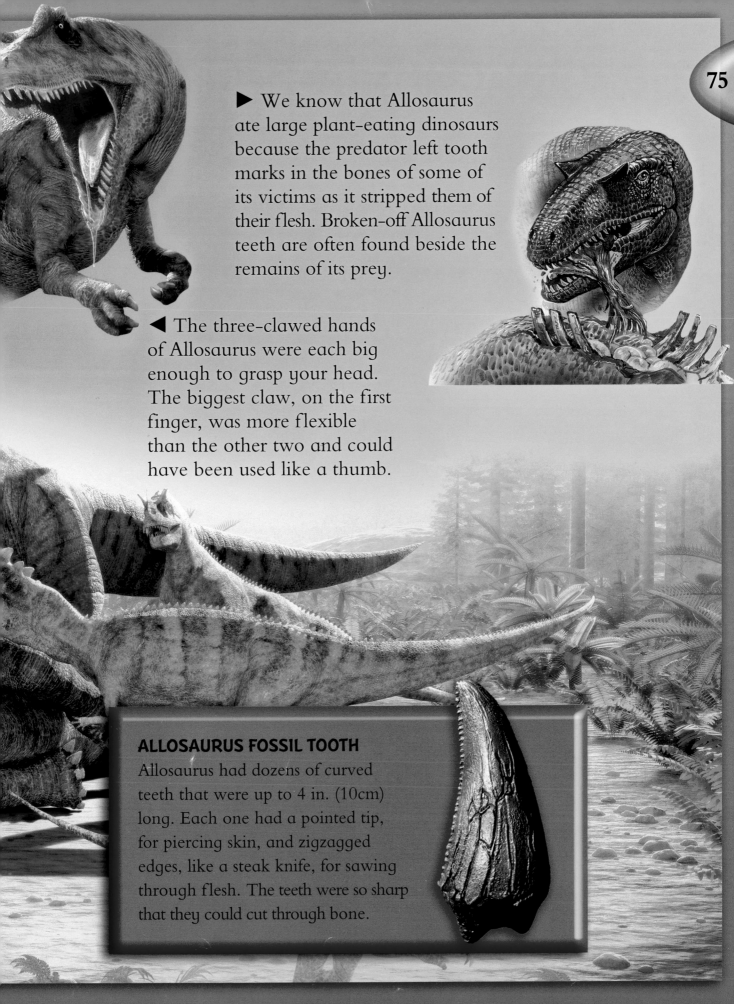

▶ We know that Allosaurus ate large plant-eating dinosaurs because the predator left tooth marks in the bones of some of its victims as it stripped them of their flesh. Broken-off Allosaurus teeth are often found beside the remains of its prey.

◀ The three-clawed hands of Allosaurus were each big enough to grasp your head. The biggest claw, on the first finger, was more flexible than the other two and could have been used like a thumb.

ALLOSAURUS FOSSIL TOOTH

Allosaurus had dozens of curved teeth that were up to 4 in. (10cm) long. Each one had a pointed tip, for piercing skin, and zigzagged edges, like a steak knife, for sawing through flesh. The teeth were so sharp that they could cut through bone.

INTERNET LINKS: www.bbc.co.uk/nature/life/Allosaurus

The biggest dinosaurs

The true giants of the dinosaur world were the plant-eating sauropods. Many different types of sauropods lived alongside one another. We know this because the fossils of more than a dozen species were found together in the rocks of the Morrison Formation in the western United States.

RIVAL FOSSIL HUNTERS

Most of the Morrison Formation sauropods were found by the fossil hunters Edward Drinker Cope and Othniel Charles Marsh. Between the 1870s and 1890s, they tried to outdo each other to find the most and best fossils.

Cope   Marsh

◄ Different types of sauropods could live together because they ate different kinds of plants. The shorter sauropods fed on low plants. The taller sauropods browsed high in the trees.

▼ This parade of sauropods includes many of the giants. They vary in length from the 56-ft.(17-m)-long Sauroposeidon to the 197-ft. (60m)-long Amphicoelias. Some of the sauropods may have weighed up to ten times more than today's elephants. Argentinosaurus may have been the heaviest.

■ Argentinosaurus
■ Supersaurus
■ Sauroposeidon
■ Amphicoelias
■ Bruhathkayosaurus
■ Diplodocus

WHICH SAUROPOD WAS THE BIGGEST?
We think Amphicoelias was the longest, but we know this dinosaur from one vertebra. The largest complete skeletons are Brachiosaurus and Diplodocus.

INTERNET LINKS: www.bbc.co.uk/nature/life/Argentinosaurus

The long ones

Some of the Late Jurassic sauropods, such as Diplodocus and Apatosaurus, were the longest land animals that ever lived. Scientists do not know exactly how long they were. We can put their backbones end to end and measure them that way. But we cannot measure the cartilage that would have been in between the bones.

Diplodocus

Apatosaurus

▲ An African elephant seems small and short when it is compared with Apatosaurus. But even this dinosaur seems short when it is shown standing beside Diplodocus.

SAUROPOD FOOTPRINTS

Scientists once thought that the sauropods needed to live in water to support the weight of their huge bodies. But sauropod footprints in rocks that formed on land prove that the land is where they lived.

▶ Diplodocus lashed its tail like a whip if it needed to defend itself against predators. The tail made a deafening sound that would scare away the sauropod's enemies. It might even have ripped off their skin.

VOCABULARY

cartilage
Tough tissue found in joints and in the soft parts of skeletons. It is not preserved in fossils.

support
To hold the weight of something.

?

WHY IS APATOSAURUS CALLED BRONTOSAURUS IN OLD BOOKS?
Apatosaurus and Brontosaurus turned out to be the same animal. It was actually named Apatosaurus first, so this name was kept.

INTERNET LINKS: www.kids-dinosaurs.com/diplodocus.html

The tallest of all

Some of the sauropods, including Giraffatitan, Sauroposeidon, and Brachiosaurus, were the tallest animals that ever lived. They walked on four legs like other sauropods. But unlike other sauropods and most other dinosaurs, their front legs were longer than their back legs. These, along with their very long and upright necks, gave them a giraffelike posture.

WHICH SAUROPOD WAS THE TALLEST?
Sauroposeidon, from Late Jurassic North America, would have stood 60 ft. (18m) tall, making it the tallest creature ever to have walked on Earth.

▲ In the early 1900s, the German scientist Werner Janensch excavated a Giraffatitan in Tanzania in Africa. He thought it was a Brachiosaurus. It has since been decided that Brachiosaurus never lived in Africa.

▶ The largest assembled skeleton in the world is that of a Giraffatitan found by Janensch. This 42-ft. (12.7m)-tall exhibit towers over people visiting the Humboldt Museum in Berlin, Germany.

SIMILAR LIFESTYLE TO GIRAFFES

Modern giraffes have front legs that are longer than their hind legs, like the tallest sauropods. The long front legs prop up the giraffe's shoulders high above its hips. A giraffe's high shoulders and upright neck lift its head higher off the ground than that of any other living animal.

▼ Brachiosaurus, from Late Jurassic North America, had high shoulders and an upright neck. These features gave this sauropod access to treetop leaves that sauropods with low-slung necks could not reach.

AMAZING!

The 4-ft. (1.2-m)-long neck bones of Sauroposeidon were unearthed in Oklahoma, in 1994. At first, scientists thought they were fossilized trees because they were so big.

Beaked dinosaurs

The giant sauropods were not the only plant-eating dinosaurs living in the Late Jurassic. A group of small ornithopods were feeding in the undergrowth at this time. These ornithopods had toothless beaks in their top and bottom jaws. The earliest, including Dryosaurus, were light. Later ones were much bigger and heavier.

?

WHERE DID DRYOSAURUS LIVE?
Dryosaurus fossils have been found in North America, Africa, and Europe. The dinosaur's name means "tree lizard." It was given this name because it lived in woodlands.

▶ Dryosaurus was lean and light. It could probably dart from side to side quickly to avoid predators. This dinosaur was also a fast sprinter. Its speed and agility was its only defense against its meat-eating enemies.

▶ The ornithopods in the first half of the Jurassic had teeth at the tip of their top jaws. Dryosaurus did not have these teeth. Its toothless upper and lower beak had sharp cutting edges instead. These beaks were ideal for snipping off food from plants.

AMAZING!

Adult Dryosaurus had short and slim arms. Dryosaurus hatchlings had larger arms in relation to their body size. This could mean that the young used their arms for walking. So while young Dryosaurus walked on all fours, the adults walked on two legs.

Cheek pouch

VOCABULARY

hatchling
A very young animal that has recently hatched from its egg.

joint
The place where two or more bones in an animal's body meet.

▲ Like earlier ornithopods, Dryosaurus had cheek pouches at the sides of its mouth. The pouches held on to food as the dinosaur chewed it. Moving joints in this creature's jaws pushed its cheeks in and out. This allowed the teeth in the top jaw to grind against the teeth in the bottom jaw.

83

Plated dinosaurs

The stegosaurs flourished in the Late Jurassic. By this time, the group included Kentrosaurus from East Africa, Stegosaurus from North America, and Miragaia from Portugal. They were bulky creatures that needed to eat huge amounts of plants to keep them going.

VOCABULARY

blood vessel
A tube that carries blood from one part of the body to another.

solar panel
A panel that aborbs the heat from the Sun, for example to heat water.

AMAZING!
Miragaia had at least 17 vertebrae in its neck. This is more than most of the sauropods had in their necks, even though Miragaia's neck was much shorter than theirs.

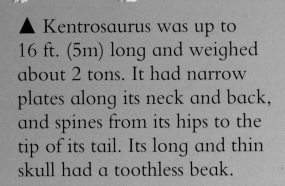

▲ Kentrosaurus was up to 16 ft. (5m) long and weighed about 2 tons. It had narrow plates along its neck and back, and spines from its hips to the tip of its tail. Its long and thin skull had a toothless beak.

▼ Miragaia had an unusually long neck for a stegosaur. The neck made this creature look part stegosaur and part sauropod. It is not yet known why Miragaia had such a long neck.

DINOSAUR PLATES

The plates may have acted like solar panels. They contained a network of blood vessels. These may have absorbed heat from the Sun. But it is possible the plates were for defense, making the dinosaur look larger than it was.

WHY DID DIFFERENT SPECIES HAVE DIFFERENT STYLES OF PLATES?

A stegosaur could recognize another member of its own species by the shape of the plates and how they were arranged.

INTERNET LINKS: www.dinosaurfact.net/jurassic/Miragaialongicollum.php

Stegosaurus

Stegosaurus was the largest of all the stegosaurs. It was up to 30 ft. (9m) long and 8 ft. (2.5m) tall at the hips. This is about the size of a bus. The first Stegosaurus fossil was found in Colorado in 1876. Since then, many Stegosaurus fossils have been found in North America.

▼ Stegosaurus had two rows of triangular-shaped plates running along its back. The plates made the dinosaur look much bigger than it actually was. This probably helped scare off predators.

VOCABULARY

flanks
The sides of an animal's body between the hips and the ribs.

spikes
Thin, pointed pieces of bone and horn.

STEGOSAURUS TEETH

Stegosaurus used its beak to snip off food from plants and trees. The dinosaur had small, ridged teeth (right) along the sides of its jaws. These crushed and shredded the plant food before the dinosaur swallowed it.

▶ There were two pairs of sharp spikes sticking out of the end of Stegosaurus's tail. These made the tail a useful weapon. By whipping its tail from side to side, a Stegosaurus could rip into a large enemy's flanks and legs.

Creative corner

Decorate a potato with Stegosaurus plates

Make a potato look bigger and fiercer! Cut out some triangular Stegosaurus plate shapes from cardboard. Now stick them into a potato and look at it from a distance. See how much bigger they make the potato look? Stegosaurus's plates would have had the same effect.

Swimming reptiles

The Late Jurassic seas were full of large reptiles. The largest of these were a group of short-necked plesiosaurs called pliosaurs. These were the top predators. They fed on ichthyosaurs and crocodiles, which in turn fed on smaller creatures such as fish and squid.

WHY WERE THE PLIOSAURS' EYES ON TOP OF THEIR HEADS?
The position of the eyes allowed pliosaurs to spot prey swimming above them. When a victim came near, the hunter launched itself upward in a surprise attack.

▼ Late Jurassic pliosaurs were certainly big enough to attack other predators such as ichthyosaurs. The pliosaurs used their sharp teeth to grab and then tear up their prey.

VOCABULARY

pliosaurs
Sea reptiles with large, flat bodies, limbs like paddles, and short tails.

squid
A sea animal with a long, soft body and ten tentacles, or arms.

▼ Geosaurus probably spent most of its life in the sea. This crocodile had far fewer scales than the land crocodiles had. Its legs and arms were shaped like paddles, and it had a fin on its tail. These features helped geosaurus move through the water easily.

AMAZING!

The German paleontologist Eberhard Fraas gave Geosaurus its name. It means "earth lizard." From its name you would think the crocodile lived on the land, but it actually lived in the sea.

TOP PREDATOR

Killer whales are the top hunters in the oceans today. Like the pliosaurs, killer whales have no natural predators. They prey on fish and larger sea animals, much like the pliosaurs did. They also have sharp teeth for trapping their prey.

Flying reptiles

Some of the best pterosaur fossils were found in Germany. They come from an area that was covered by a lagoon in the Late Jurassic. At this time, there were about six types of pterosaurs hunting for fish in the lagoon. We can tell what pterosaurs ate from the shape of their jaws and teeth.

AMAZING!

Pterosaurs could fly like birds, but they did not walk like birds. Fossil footprints show that they walked on all fours. They used their wing-hands to stop themselves from toppling forward.

▶ A flock of Pterodactylus head out across the lagoon to find fish. A pair of Rhamphorhynchus use their outstretched wings to glide through the air. Two Ctenochasma sit on the shore and wait for their wings to dry.

PTEROSAUR JAWS

Dsungaripterus, from the Cretaceous, had curved, pointed jaws for eating shellfish. Dimorphodon, from the Triassic, had different sizes of teeth in its jaws for eating a variety of prey. Ornithocheirus, from the Cretaceous, had bumps on its jaws to keep it stable in the air as it fished with its beak under the water.

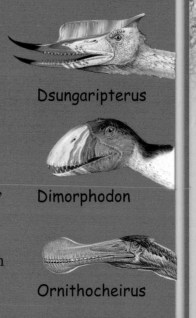

Dsungaripterus

Dimorphodon

Ornithocheirus

◄ Some of the pterosaur fossils found in Germany show the impression of the wings as well as the delicate bones. Some fossils even show that the pterosaur's body was covered with hair.

Creative corner

Make a pterosaur kite

Tape drinking straws together to make a cross-shaped frame. Draw a pterosaur on diamond-shaped paper and tape it onto the frame. Tie a long piece of string to the center.

INTERNET LINKS: www.abc.net.au/dinosaurs/fact_files/sea/rhamphor.htm

They all lived together

The rocks of the Morrison Formation in the western United States formed in the Late Jurassic. They are made of layers of sediments that were laid down by rivers. The rocks are rich in animal and plant fossils. These show us what life was like in North America in the Late Jurassic.

▼ In Late Jurassic North America, herds of Apatosaurus walked among horsetails and ferns on the river plains. Allosaurus was the top predator. It preyed on Stegosaurus, as did Ornitholestes.

CAN YOU FIND?
1. Stegosaurus
2. Allosaurus
3. Ornitholestes
4. Apatosaurus
5. Ferns

MORRISON FORMATION ANIMALS

The Morrison Formation animals include many shrewlike mammals. They had sharp teeth that looked a little like needles. These teeth were ideal for catching prey such as insects and beetles.

VOCABULARY

sediments
Particles deposited, or laid down, by water, wind, or ice.

shrew
A tiny insect-eating mammal that looks a little like a mouse.

▼ Scientists figure out the age of fossils by looking at rock layers. The oldest fossils lie in the bottom layers. The youngest fossils sit at the top. This is because new sediments are always laid on top of older ones.

Drifting dinosaurs

When the dinosaurs first appeared in the Triassic, all of the land on Earth was joined together. Over time, the land split apart into the continents we know today. Related dinosaurs became cut off from one another by the seas. Gradually, new species of dinosaurs evolved on each continent.

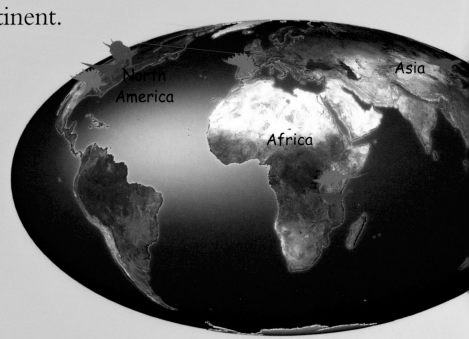

▶ This map of the modern world shows where the fossils of certain dinosaurs have been discovered. Dinosaurs shown in the same colors here are related to one another.

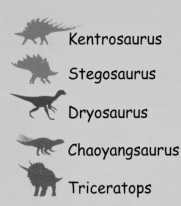

Kentrosaurus

Stegosaurus

Dryosaurus

Chaoyangsaurus

Triceratops

▶ Dryosaurus is from the Late Jurassic. Fossils belonging to this species are found in Africa and North America. These fossil finds prove that the two continents were once joined together.

◀ At the very beginning of the Jurassic period, Africa and South America were joined together. A strip of land connected the continents of North America and South America.

Kentrosaurus

▶ Kentrosaurus and Stegosaurus are closely related. Their ancestors were able to roam Africa and North America when they were one landmass. Today, the continents—and the fossils of the two dinosaur species—are separated by the Atlantic Ocean.

Stegosaurus

Triceratops

HOW DID THE CONTINENTS DRIFT APART?

Earth's rocky surface is divided into plates. These fit together like a jigsaw puzzle and move very slowly. Oceans form in the gaps created when the plates pull apart.

◀ Chaoyangsaurus, from Late Jurassic China, is an ancestor of Triceratops, from Late Cretaceous North America. Their relatives spread from China into North America at a time when the regions were joined together.

Chaoyangsaurus

Now you know!

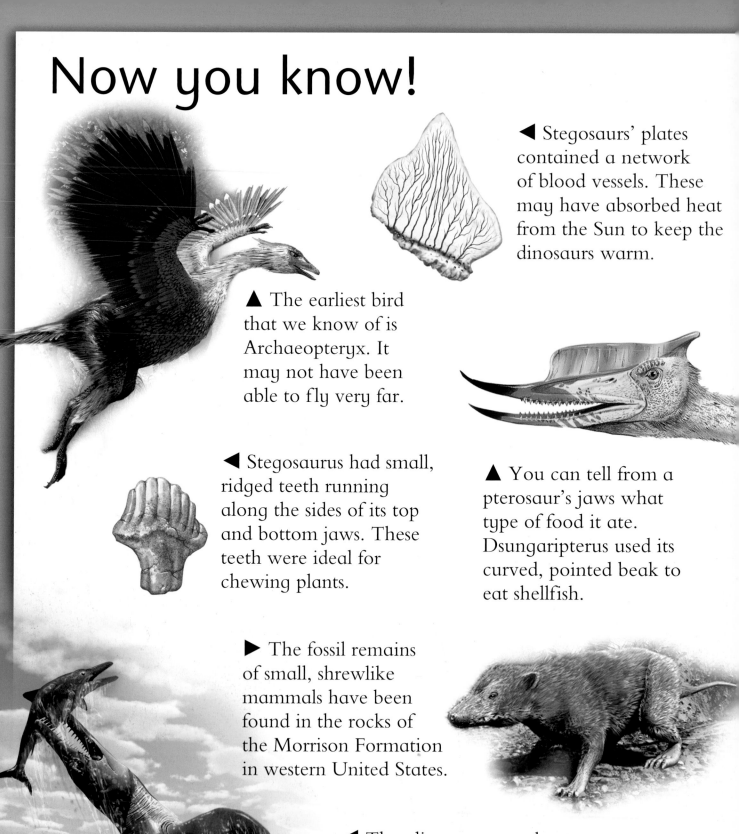

◀ Stegosaurs' plates contained a network of blood vessels. These may have absorbed heat from the Sun to keep the dinosaurs warm.

▲ The earliest bird that we know of is Archaeopteryx. It may not have been able to fly very far.

◀ Stegosaurus had small, ridged teeth running along the sides of its top and bottom jaws. These teeth were ideal for chewing plants.

▲ You can tell from a pterosaur's jaws what type of food it ate. Dsungaripterus used its curved, pointed beak to eat shellfish.

▶ The fossil remains of small, shrewlike mammals have been found in the rocks of the Morrison Formation in western United States.

◀ The pliosaurs were the top predators in the Late Jurassic seas. They were big enough to snap up and eat large prey such as ichthyosaurs.

A variety of dinosaurs

The Early Cretaceous began about 145 million years ago. During this period, the different continents began to develop their own unique dinosaurs. There were feathered dinosaurs in China and dinosaurs with sails on their backs in Africa. The stegosaurs had almost gone, and the sauropods were beginning to die out. Now the main plant-eating dinosaurs were ornithopods with ducklike beaks.

The Cretaceous world

The Early Cretaceous was very warm, and there were wet and dry seasons. Flowering plants first appeared at this time. Dinosaurs became more plentiful, and more types evolved. Unlike in earlier periods, Cretaceous dinosaurs developed differently in different areas.

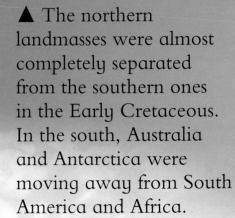

▲ The northern landmasses were almost completely separated from the southern ones in the Early Cretaceous. In the south, Australia and Antarctica were moving away from South America and Africa.

CAN YOU FIND?
1. A dinosaur with a sail on its back
2. A large crocodile
3. A flying reptile

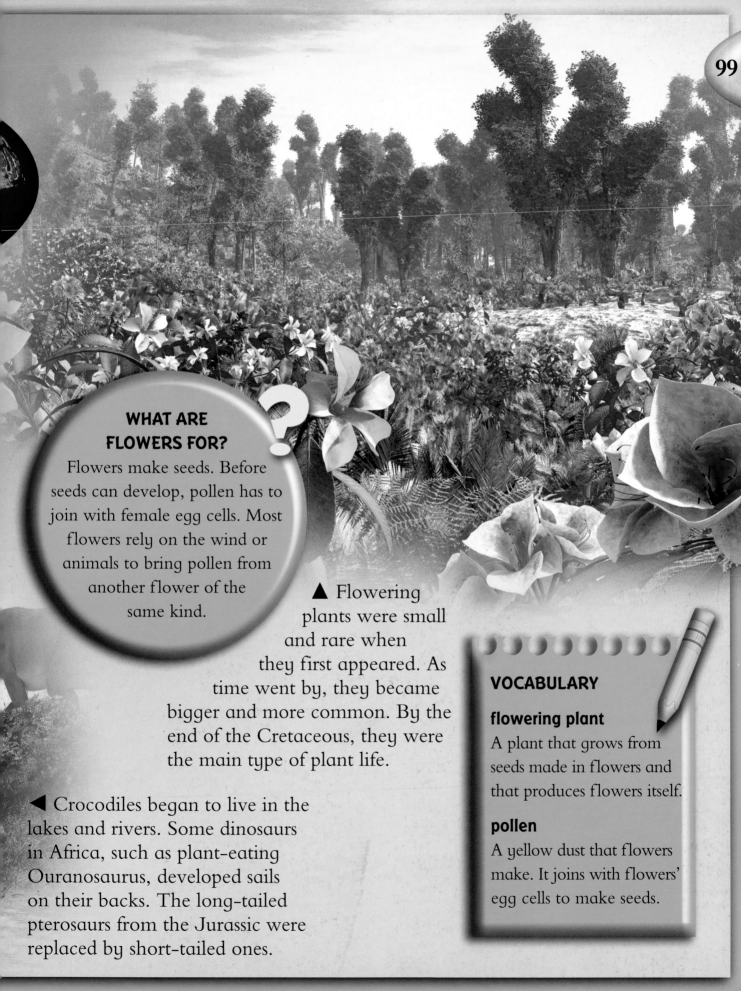

WHAT ARE FLOWERS FOR?

Flowers make seeds. Before seeds can develop, pollen has to join with female egg cells. Most flowers rely on the wind or animals to bring pollen from another flower of the same kind.

▲ Flowering plants were small and rare when they first appeared. As time went by, they became bigger and more common. By the end of the Cretaceous, they were the main type of plant life.

◄ Crocodiles began to live in the lakes and rivers. Some dinosaurs in Africa, such as plant-eating Ouranosaurus, developed sails on their backs. The long-tailed pterosaurs from the Jurassic were replaced by short-tailed ones.

VOCABULARY

flowering plant
A plant that grows from seeds made in flowers and that produces flowers itself.

pollen
A yellow dust that flowers make. It joins with flowers' egg cells to make seeds.

INTERNET LINKS: www.dinosaurfact.net/Cretaceous.php

Feathered dinosaurs

Until the 1990s, scientists thought that all dinosaurs had scaly skin. Then, in 1995, a Cretaceous dinosaur with feathers was discovered in rocks in northeast China. The rocks are known as the Jehol group. Since 1995, many more feathered dinosaurs have been found in these rocks.

AMAZING!
The feathered dinosaurs found in China must be relatives of birds. But they appeared later than the first bird, Archaeopteryx. They could have been early birds that lost their power of flight.

▲ Sinosauropteryx was the first feathered dinosaur ever found. There were feathers along its tail and over its back. This fossil find made scientists wonder if it meant that other dinosaurs had feathers.

◀ Protarchaeopteryx's arm feathers looked like those of modern flightless birds. Details in the fossil skeleton show that it could not flap its arms. For these reasons, it is unlikely that this creature could fly.

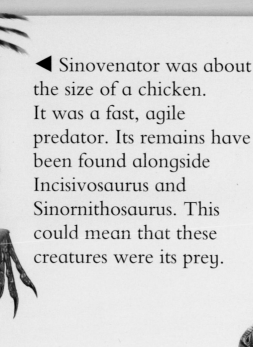

◀ Sinovenator was about the size of a chicken. It was a fast, agile predator. Its remains have been found alongside Incisivosaurus and Sinornithosaurus. This could mean that these creatures were its prey.

▼ Incisivosaurus was a goofy-looking creature with big front teeth. The teeth were not sharp, so perhaps this dinosaur was a plant eater. It could have used the teeth to snatch up tough plant stems.

?

WHY DID THESE DINOSAURS HAVE FEATHERS?
The feathers kept the dinosaurs warm and dry. Like modern birds, the dinosaurs probably used their more showy feathers for display.

◀ Sinornithosaurus had long, birdlike feathers on its arms. But this creature was a dinosaur and could not fly. Scientists do not yet know what its wings were for.

INTERNET LINKS: www.bbc.co.uk/news/science-environment-14941647

The bird connection

Of all the feathered dinosaurs found in China, Caudipteryx is the closest known relative of birds. This creature was a mix of both kinds of animals. It had birdlike feathers, a short head with a beak, and a short tail. But it had the teeth and many of the bones of a theropod.

VOCABULARY

plume
A large, colorful feather used by a bird for display.

quill
The hollow stem of a feather.

FEATHER EVOLUTION

(1) Scales on the skin developed into bristles.
(2) These became fluffy to keep the dinosaur warm.
(3) Later ones were fluffier.
(4) The first display feathers had a quill in the center.
(5) They were shaped a little like the flight feathers of birds.

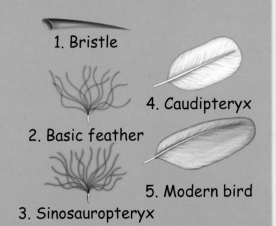

1. Bristle

4. Caudipteryx

2. Basic feather

5. Modern bird

3. Sinosauropteryx

Sinosauropteryx

Caudipteryx

◀ Sinosauropteryx had short, fluffy body feathers to keep it warm. Caudipteryx had similar body feathers, but it also had long plumes on its arms and tail. It may have been more birdlike than Sinosauropteryx was, but it was not able to fly.

▼ Caudipteryx was about the size of a turkey. It had powerful, long legs and a light body, so it was probably a fast runner. Unlike birds, this creature had teeth at the front of its upper beak.

AMAZING!
Birds are living dinosaurs. Feathers developed on land-living dinosaurs long before birds were able to fly. This means that modern birds developed from dinosaurs.

Creative corner

Start a collection of bird feathers

Use sketches of feathers that you see (but do not touch) to make a poster showing the different types. They all have a job to do. Fluffy ones keep the bird warm. Long, colorful ones are for showing off. Wide, flat ones are used for flying.

Four-winged dinosaur

Microraptor was a dinosaur that took to the skies. This crow-sized creature had curved claws that were ideal for climbing trees. It had four wings, but it could not flap them to fly. It used them to glide from tree to tree instead. Microraptor fossils are found in the Jehol group of rocks in China.

AMAZING!

The fossil of what appeared to be a flying dinosaur was unveiled in 1999. Known as Archaeoraptor, it turned out to be a fake. The fossil was made from a Microraptor tail added to the fossil skeleton of an early bird.

▲ Microraptor scrambled up trees using its claws. It then spread out its arms and legs to form two pairs of wings and glided from tree to tree. Microraptor may have used its feathered tail for steering through the air.

► The fossils of Microraptor are so well preserved that they show almost every detail of this creature's body. Flight feathers can be seen on each arm and each leg. There are also flight feathers on the tail.

BIPLANE

Early airplanes had two pairs of wings. One set sat above the other. This gave the plane more lift as it flew. Microraptor may have held its front wings higher than its hind wings for the same effect.

VOCABULARY

fake
Something that is not real or genuine.

territory
An area defended by an animal or animals against other animals of the same sex or species.

▼ This pair of Microraptors may be flashing their feathers at each other in a fight for territory. Microraptor's long feathers would have made it clumsy on the ground, making it easy for predators to catch it.

INTERNET LINKS: www.utexas.edu/know/2012/03/08/microraptor_dinosaurs_birds/

Small meat eaters

The fiercest animals of the Early Cretaceous were small, aggressive hunting dinosaurs such as Deinonychus. Their jaws were full of sharp teeth, and deadly claws sprouted from their toes. Fine down protected their bodies from the cold. They also had longer feathers for showing off.

AMAZING!
Scientists who examined the feet and leg bones of Deinonychus have figured out that it could run at speeds of up to 28 mph (45km/h). This is faster than the fastest man on Earth.

VICIOUS CLAW
Deinonychus had huge claws on each of its second toes. They were twice as long as any of their other claws. The claw could rise, ready to flick forward and slice open prey.

▶ Deinonychus stalked large plant-eating dinosaurs such as Tenontosaurus. The hunters worked in packs. They took down their prey by leaping on their backs and attacking them with their claws and teeth.

◄ Mei lived in Early Cretaceous China. The fossil of this duck-sized creature shows it curled up with its head tucked under its winglike arm. It had died in volcanic ash and was buried by it.

▲ Dilong was about the size of a turkey. It is an ancestor of the king of all dinosaurs, Tyrannosaurus. Dilong's body was covered in fine, feathery down. This has led many scientists to wonder if Tyrannosaurus also had feathers.

VOCABULARY

aggressive
Ready or likely to attack.

down
Fine, soft, fuzzy feathers. They keep an animal warm.

INTERNET LINKS: www.sciencekids.co.nz/sciencefacts/dinosaurs/deinonychus.html

Fish-eating dinosaurs

A small group of Cretaceous theropods may have hunted fish. Their skulls were similar to the skulls of modern fish-eating crocodiles. They also had large, curved thumb claws that they may have used as fishhooks. The skeleton of one of these dinosaurs, Baryonyx, was found with fish scales inside it.

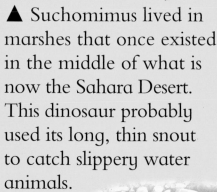

▲ Suchomimus lived in marshes that once existed in the middle of what is now the Sahara Desert. This dinosaur probably used its long, thin snout to catch slippery water animals.

▼ Baryonyx may have waded out into rivers and streams to catch its prey. When a fish came near, the dinosaur probably hooked it out of the water using its thumb claw.

▶ We know that modern grizzly bears can sweep salmon from rivers with their claws. So it is possible that the fish-eating dinosaurs also caught their prey in this way.

AMAZING!
Baryonyx had almost twice the number of teeth that most other theropods had. There were 64 teeth in its bottom jaw and 32 teeth in its top one. All of these teeth were probably great for catching and holding on to this fish eater's scaly prey.

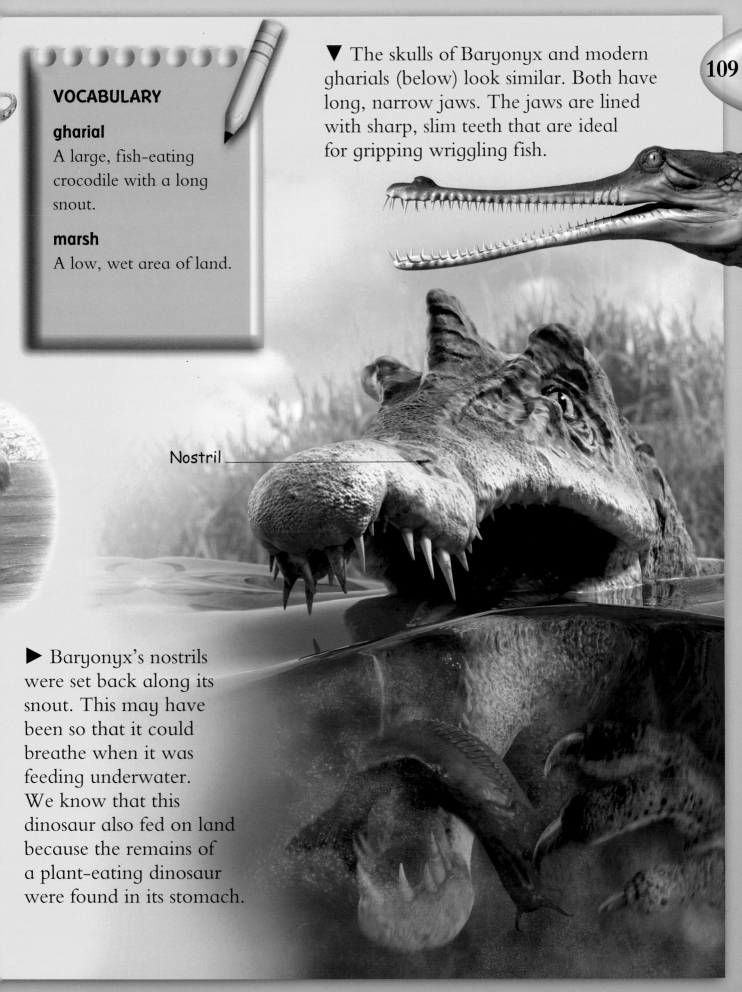

VOCABULARY

gharial
A large, fish-eating crocodile with a long snout.

marsh
A low, wet area of land.

▼ The skulls of Baryonyx and modern gharials (below) look similar. Both have long, narrow jaws. The jaws are lined with sharp, slim teeth that are ideal for gripping wriggling fish.

Nostril

▶ Baryonyx's nostrils were set back along its snout. This may have been so that it could breathe when it was feeding underwater. We know that this dinosaur also fed on land because the remains of a plant-eating dinosaur were found in its stomach.

INTERNET LINKS: www.nhm.ac.uk/kids-only/dinosaurs/finding-baryonyx/index.html

Scythe dinosaurs

Strange-looking, bipedal dinosaurs with feathers and long, scythe-shaped claws lived throughout Early and Late Cretaceous times. Their wrist and toe bones prove that they were theropods. But their teeth and hip bones show that they were plant eaters.

AMAZING!
Therizinosaurus's claws were about 3 ft. (1m) long. Scientists thought that they belonged to a giant sloth or turtle when they were first found in Mongolia in 1953.

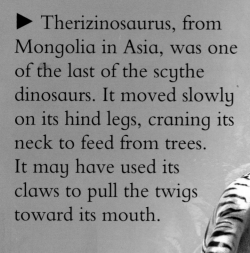

▶ Therizinosaurus, from Mongolia in Asia, was one of the last of the scythe dinosaurs. It moved slowly on its hind legs, craning its neck to feed from trees. It may have used its claws to pull the twigs toward its mouth.

SKULL AND HIPS

The scythe dinosaurs used the beaks at the front of their jaws for nipping plants. Small, blunt teeth in their cheeks ground up the food. Unusually for theropods, their hip bones were swept back to allow room for their large stomachs. They needed these to digest the huge amount of plants that they ate.

Hip bones

Skull

▲ The only known fossil remains of Deinocheirus are a pair of massive arms and fragments of its ribs and vertebrae. The arms are about 8 ft. (2.5m) in length, and the claws are up to 12 in. (30cm) long.

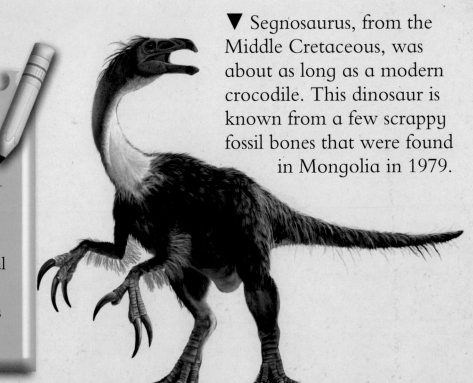

▼ Segnosaurus, from the Middle Cretaceous, was about as long as a modern crocodile. This dinosaur is known from a few scrappy fossil bones that were found in Mongolia in 1979.

VOCABULARY

scythe
A tool with a long, curved blade.

sloth
A slow-moving mammal that lives in trees. Sloths are related to armadillos and anteaters.

Heavy dinosaurs

The sauropods of the Cretaceous period included some of the heaviest creatures ever to walk on Earth. Fossilized skin found with the skeletons of these long-necked, plant-eating dinosaurs show that some of them had body armor. Cretaceous sauropods have been found on all of the continents of the world.

► Saltasaurus had bony studs set in the skin of its back and sides. These dinosaurs lived in herds. We know this because hundreds of their nests were preserved together at one site in Argentina.

◄ Saltasaurus mothers dug holes in the ground and then laid their eggs and buried them with soil and plants. There were about 25 eggs in each of the nests at the nesting site in Argentina. Many of the eggs contained fossilized embryos.

AMAZING!
Argentinosaurus was huge, but its eggs were only about the size of a football. The young had a lot of growing to do to reach the 121-ft. (37-m)-length of an adult. This may have taken more than 40 years.

◀ Antarctosaurus's name means "southern lizard" and refers to the continent of South America. This is where the dinosaur's fossils were first found. Others have since been found in Asia and Africa.

▶ Argentinosaurus fossils are found in rocks in South America that date to the middle of the Cretaceous. This colossal sauropod may have weighed more than 100 tons.

VOCABULARY

embryos
Animals or plants that are just starting to develop inside an egg, the mother, or a seed.

nesting site
A place where animals choose to lay their eggs.

Dinosaur Cove

Australia lay south of the Antarctic Circle during the Early Cretaceous. The dinosaurs living there had to cope with very cold winters, when the nights were long and there were very few daylight hours. The remains of some of these dinosaurs are found in Dinosaur Cove in Australia.

AUSTRALIA
Present day

AUSTRALIA
104 million years ago

ANTARCTICA
104 million years ago

▲ During the Early Cretaceous, Australia was breaking free from Antarctica and moving north. Dinosaur Cove (shown in red) was close to the South Pole at this time.

AMAZING!
Since the Early Cretaceous, Australia has moved more than 3,200 mi. (5,200km) north to its present-day position. This is almost the distance between London, England, and New York.

Timimus

Leaellynasaura

▶ Leaellynasaura's long tail and small head made it look a little like a kangaroo. It had huge eyes to find its way around in the darkness. Leaellynasaura shared the gloom with an ostrichlike meat eater called Timimus and a dinosaur called Atlascopcosaurus.

HOW DO WE KNOW THAT AUSTRALIA WAS COLD AT THIS TIME?

Some kinds of sediment are laid down only in frozen lakes. These sediments form some of the rocks in present-day Dinosaur Cove.

▲ The lakes and rivers in Early Cretaceous Dinosaur Cove would have frozen in the winter. Plants grew only during the short Antarctic summers. But there was enough food for herds of plant-eating Leaellynasaura, so there was plenty of prey for Timimus.

VOCABULARY

Antarctic Circle
An imaginary line that runs around Earth south of the equator and north of the South Pole.

South Pole
The southernmost point on Earth's surface.

Mining for fossils

The first dinosaur fossil ever found in Australia was uncovered at Dinosaur Cove in 1903. But the fossil site was not excavated properly until the 1980s. It was difficult to get to because it was halfway up a cliff. The scientists had to build platforms onto the cliff face so that they could tunnel into the rock.

VOCABULARY

dynamite
A substance that explodes. It is used to blast through rock to make tunnels.

fragment
A small part broken off or separated from something.

▼ The paleontologists used mining equipment and dynamite to tunnel into the cliff face. They also had to use heavy drills to break up the hard rock inside the tunnels so that they could get to the fossils.

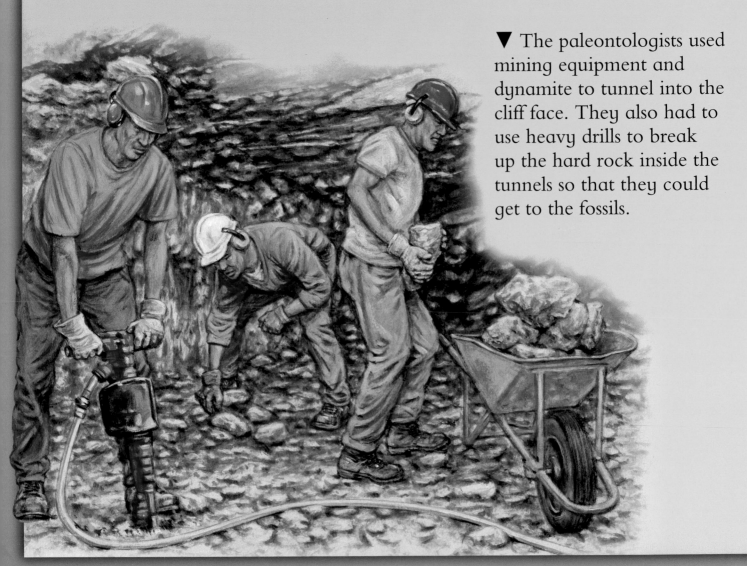

◀ Leaellynasaura was the most common dinosaur found at Dinosaur Cove. Scientists think this plant eater fed on ferns and cycads. Many fossils of these plants were found at the site.

◀ Very few meat-eating dinosaurs were found at Dinosaur Cove. One of them was Timimus. All that was found of this species were two thigh bones. They belonged to two different individuals.

▲ A jaw fragment and some teeth were all that was found of Atlascopcosaurus. These were enough for scientists to figure out that this dinosaur was a small, bipedal plant eater.

AMAZING!

Atlascopcosaurus was named after the Atlas Copco mining company. It supplied the equipment for the excavations. Leaellynasaura and Timimus were named after Leaellyn and Tim, the children of the two paleontologists that first studied the dinosaurs.

Iguanodonts

The small, swift, two-footed ornithopods of the Jurassic developed into much larger, slower dinosaurs in the Early Cretaceous. Most of these new dinosaurs, known as iguanodonts, were too heavy to walk on only their hind legs, so they went on all fours. But they could still rear up on their back legs to reach food.

VOCABULARY

camouflage
A way of hiding something by coloring or covering it so that it blends in with its surroundings.

muted
Colors that are soft and dull, not bright and strong.

▼ Ouranosaurus roamed Africa in Early Cretaceous times. This iguanodont had a sail along its back and tail, supported by wide spines from its backbone. The sail may have absorbed heat from the Sun to warm up the dinosaur. But it could have been used for display instead.

CAMOUFLAGE

We cannot be sure what color Iguanodon was. It seems likely, though, that it needed to blend in with its surroundings to hide from hungry meat eaters. It was probably covered in greens and browns similar to those found in the woodlands in which it lived.

▼ Tenontosaurus was up to 26 ft. (8m) long. Its large size probably scared off predators, except when the predators hunted in packs. Tenontosaurus was a North American relative of Iguanodon.

▼ We know that Iguanodon moved around in herds because of a fossil site in Belgium. A group of young and old Iguanodon was discovered in a coal mine there in the 1870s. Trackways that were probably made by herds of Iguanodon have been found in other places.

Creative corner

Use camouflage to play hide-and-seek

(1) Wear clothing in muted colors with no bold logos. Use face paints to blur your face. (2) Decorate a cap with items from your surroundings and cover up your hair with it. (3) Move quietly and slowly.

1 2 3

INTERNET LINKS: www.abc.net.au/beasts/playground/camouflage.htm

Iguanodon

Iguanodon fossils are found in Asia, Europe, and North America. This Early Cretaceous, plant-eating dinosaur had birdlike feet with three toes. It used its five-fingered hands as weapons, for walking on, and for feeding.

▼ Hundreds of Iguanodon traveled together. They fed on the move, using their hands to grasp plants and their beaks to nip them. The dinosaurs' arms were long enough to reach to the ground, so they probably walked on all fours.

AMAZING!

Iguanodon was the second dinosaur ever named. It was first described in 1825 by the English doctor Gideon Mantell. He had found Iguanodon teeth in Sussex, England, three years earlier.

FOOTPRINTS

These footprints were probably made by an Iguanodon. They show the triangular prints that this dinosaur's three-toed feet would make.

VOCABULARY

conical
Cone-shaped.

flexible
Able to bend without
breaking.

▶ Iguanodon used a
conical spike on its hand
as a weapon. The dinosaur
walked on its three chunky
middle fingers. It used its thin,
flexible fifth fingers as we
would use our thumbs.

The Cretaceous sea

The oceans swarmed with marine reptiles right up until the end of the Cretaceous. The plesiosaurs continued to stalk the seas, but the ichthyosaurs died out early in the period. They were replaced by giant reptiles called mosasaurs. Sea turtles did well throughout the Cretaceous period.

AMAZING!

In 1868, Edward Drinker Cope became the first person to assemble an Elasmosaurus skeleton. He put the head on the wrong end, thinking that the long neck was the creature's tail.

▼ Elasmosaurus swam near the surface of the water. Its neck had more than 70 vertebrae, making it the longest neck of any plesiosaur. Elasmosaurus used its long neck to stretch to passing prey.

ELASMOSAURUS HEAD

Like most long-necked plesiosaurs, Elasmosaurus had a tiny head. Its sharp teeth pointed outward. The top and bottom set of teeth interlinked to form a deadly fish trap.

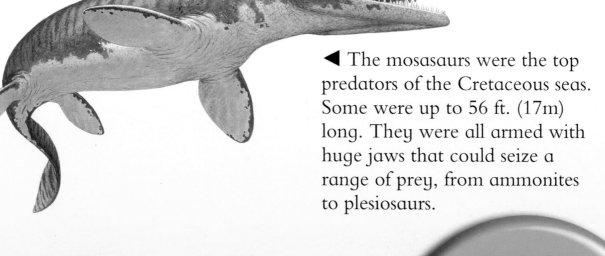

◀ The mosasaurs were the top predators of the Cretaceous seas. Some were up to 56 ft. (17m) long. They were all armed with huge jaws that could seize a range of prey, from ammonites to plesiosaurs.

▼ Archelon swam in the Early Cretaceous seas that covered part of North America. It was 16 ft. (5m) wide from flipper tip to flipper tip, making it the biggest turtle that ever existed. Its massive, powerful paddles helped it swim very fast.

WHERE DID ARCHELON SPEND ITS TIME?

It spent most of its time in the sea, possibly sleeping on the surface for several months of the year. It would have returned to land only to mate and lay its eggs.

The Cretaceous sky

The skies were filled with pterosaurs during the Cretaceous period. Some of these reptiles such as Quetzalcoatlus, grew very large. But birds began to crowd out the pterosaurs at the end of the Cretaceous. These birds had developed from land-based feathered dinosaurs, not pterosaurs.

Pterodaustro, from Early Cretaceous Argentina and Chile

CRETACEOUS BIRD

Confuciusornis was one of the most common birds in the Early Cretaceous skies. Female Confuciusornis had short tails. But the male birds had long tails with feathers on the ends. These looked liked streamers, and it is likely that the male birds used them to show off.

▲ Unlike other pterosaurs, Quetzalcoatlus may have stalked prey inland. Pterodaustro was a filter feeder, like the modern flamingo. Tapejara used its downward-curving beak to pluck fish from the sea. Cearadactylus trapped fish with its teeth.

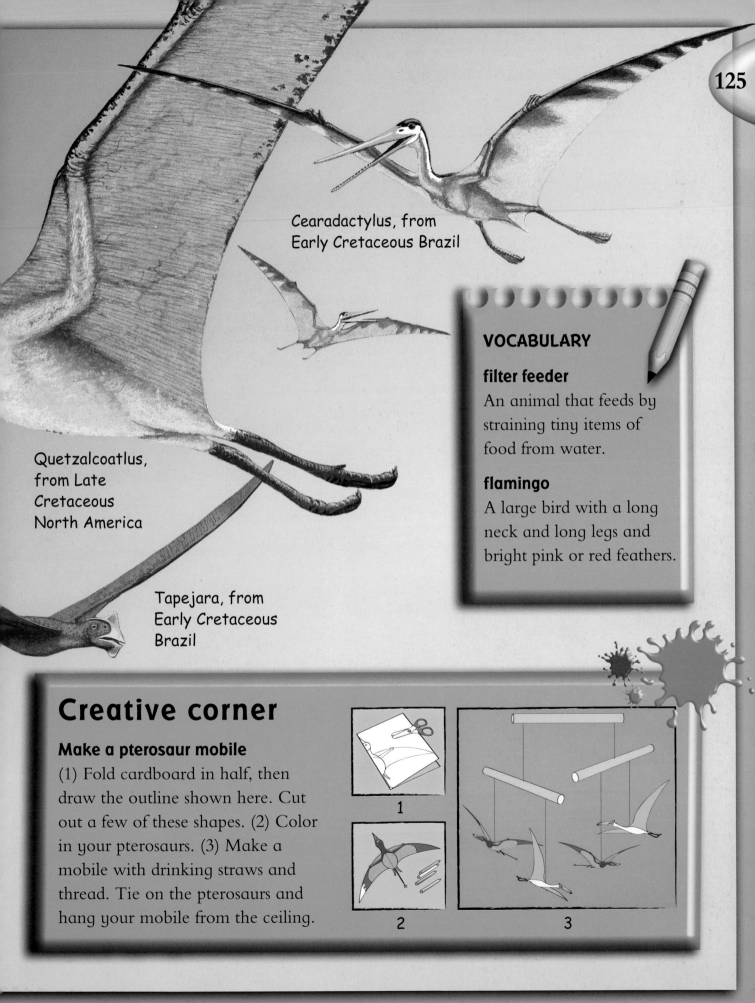

Cearadactylus, from
Early Cretaceous Brazil

Quetzalcoatlus,
from Late
Cretaceous
North America

Tapejara, from
Early Cretaceous
Brazil

VOCABULARY

filter feeder
An animal that feeds by
straining tiny items of
food from water.

flamingo
A large bird with a long
neck and long legs and
bright pink or red feathers.

Creative corner

Make a pterosaur mobile

(1) Fold cardboard in half, then
draw the outline shown here. Cut
out a few of these shapes. (2) Color
in your pterosaurs. (3) Make a
mobile with drinking straws and
thread. Tie on the pterosaurs and
hang your mobile from the ceiling.

1

2

3

Getting it wrong

New dinosaur fossil discoveries are being made all the time. Each one gives scientists more clues to how dinosaurs looked and behaved when they were alive. Sometimes new discoveries show that the beliefs paleontologists had about a certain species were wrong.

AMAZING!
Between the 1820s and 1880s, scientists believed that Iguanodon's large thumb spike was a horn that sat on its nose.

WHEN WAS HYPSILOPHODON FIRST FOUND?
The fossils of this plant-eating dinosaur were first discovered in 1849. They were found on the Isle of Wight, England.

▼ Scientists once thought that Hypsilophodon lived in trees and could perch on branches with curled toes like a bird. Scientists now think it was a fast runner, with feet that were well adapted for running along the ground.

▲ For a long time after it was first discovered, scientists thought that Iguanodon was a heavily built, four-legged animal with a horn on its nose.

▲ Skeletons found in Belgium in the 1880s led scientists to believe that Iguanodon walked on two legs and dragged its tail on the ground.

▲ Today, we think that Iguanodon held its tail off the ground and walked mostly on all fours. It may have walked on two legs sometimes.

◄ The arms on the second Compsognathus skeleton ever found were crushed, so scientists mistook them for flippers. Experts now believe that this dinosaur had arms instead of flippers.

Creative corner

Make an imaginary dinosaur!

Cut out the body parts of different dinosaurs and other reptiles and put them together to make your own dinosaur. It might have the head of a Triceratops, the plates of a stegosaur and the wings of a pterosaur. Make up a name for your dinosaur.

INTERNET LINKS: www.nhm.ac.uk/kids-only/dinosaurs/3d-dinos/iguanodon/index.html

Now you know!

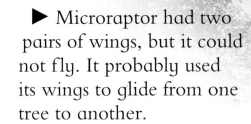

▶ Microraptor had two pairs of wings, but it could not fly. It probably used its wings to glide from one tree to another.

▲ In the Jehol group of rocks in northeast China, fossils of many dinosaurs with feathers, such as Sinornithosaurus, have been found.

▶ Baryonyx was probably a fish eater. It may have trapped fish with its teeth or hooked them out of the water using its claws.

▼ Deinonychus had large, curved claws on the second toe of each foot. They could rise and flick forward.

◀ Iguanodon had a cone-shaped claw on each hand. Scientists think that the dinosaur used these claws to defend itself.

▼ Archelon was the biggest turtle that ever lived. It swam in a sea that covered part of North America in the Early Cretaceous.

◀ It is possible that Iguanodon and other plant-eating dinosaurs had camouflage so that they could hide from their enemies.

Change and extinction

The Late Cretaceous began about 83 million years ago. It was a period of great success for the dinosaurs. Many new types appeared. The dinosaurs dominated the land right up until the end of the Cretaceous about 65 million years ago, but then they all died out suddenly. No one is certain why this happened.

The Late Cretaceous

The continents continued to move apart during the Late Cretaceous. The climate was cooler than it was before but warmer than it is today. Flowering plants spread rapidly during this time, and there was a diverse collection of dinosaurs.

North America

South America

India

▼ The plant-eating dinosaurs included duck-billed species, such as Edmontosaurus, and dinosaurs with horns, such as Triceratops. They were prey for big meat-eating dinosaurs, such as Tyrannosaurus, and large crocodiles.

Triceratops

Tyrannosaurus

VOCABULARY

diverse
Showing a great deal of variety.

duck-billed
Animals that have beaks resembling those of ducks.

◀ North and South America moved west into the Pacific Ocean. India was moving north toward Asia. Australia and Antarctica had separated and were moving closer to their present-day positions.

Asia

AMAZING!
Late Cretaceous dinosaurs came in a wide variety of shapes and sizes. There were as many different types of dinosaurs living in this period as there were in the other periods put together.

WAS THERE GRASS AT THIS TIME?
There was grass, but very little of it compared with today. We know that it existed because scientists found grass pollen in the stomach of a Late Cretaceous sauropod.

▼ Some of the trees in Late Cretaceous North America are still around today. They include birch, beech, oak, and willow trees. There was hardly any grass. Instead, the ground was covered by flowering plants.

Edmontosaurus

INTERNET LINKS: http://animals.howstuffworks.com/dinosaurs/edmontosaurus.htm

Fast and smart

In the Late Cretaceous, some dinosaurs were fast on their feet and good at eating a range of food. Struthiomimus and Oviraptor probably ate plants as well as animals, while Bambiraptor and Troodon were speedy hunters with well-developed brains.

AMAZING!
A 14-year-old boy named Wes Linster discovered the first Bambiraptor skeleton ever found. He came across the skeleton in 1995 when he was fossil hunting with his parents near Glacier National Park in Montana.

?

HOW FAST COULD STRUTHIOMIMUS RUN?
This dinosaur had powerful, muscular legs that could carry it at speeds of up to 50 mph (80km/h). This is as fast as a gazelle!

▼ Struthiomimus, from North America, probably used its top speeds to escape from large predators rather than for hunting. It fed on small animals, as well as leaves and fruit.

▶ Oviraptor, from Late Cretaceous Mongolia, had a toothless beak and powerful jaws. These suggest that it was an omnivore, which means that it ate meat and plants. The crest on its head was probably used for display.

▲ Bambiraptor had the long legs and slim build of a fast runner. One curved claw on each of its feet could rise and then flick forward with force. Its mouth was full of sharp teeth.

BRAINY DINOSAUR

Troodon, from North America, grew to 6.5 ft. (2m) long. This meat-eating dinosaur had a large brain relative to the size of its skull and its overall size. It was probably one of the smartest hunters in North America at the time. Its large eyes allowed it to see and hunt at night.

INTERNET LINKS: www.nhm.ac.uk/kids-only/dinosaurs/who-was-oviraptor/index.html

Fight to the death

Paleontologists working in the Gobi Desert in Mongolia found an amazing fossil in 1971. It shows a predator called Velociraptor wrapped around a plant-eating dinosaur, called Protoceratops. It is clear that they were fighting when they died, but scientists are not sure what killed these beasts as they struggled.

▼ The dinosaurs were preserved with the Velociraptor's left claw grasping the Protoceratops's head frill. Its right arm was clamped in the plant eater's beak. The meat eater's foot claws were curled into the plant eater's throat and stomach area.

AMAZING!

Not many dinosaurs died of old age. Some died in natural disasters or were eaten by predators. Others died in fights, starved to death, or became diseased.

◀ The Velociraptor and Protoceratops may have died in a landslide, when a mass of earth tumbled down a mountain and fell on top of them. It is also possible that they were smothered by sand during a sandstorm.

BRAVE PARENT

Protoceratops had a frill around its neck that made it look bigger, but this did not scare off the Velociraptor. So why did the plant eater stand and fight rather than run away? Many scientists believe that it may have been protecting its nest.

INTERNET LINKS: www.bbc.co.uk/nature/life/Velociraptor#p00clsng

Giant meat eaters

The most awesome of all the meat-eating dinosaurs lived in the Late Cretaceous. These giants walked heavily on their massive legs and carried their heads forward. Their muscular arms were strangely short, and they ended in tiny, two-clawed and three-clawed hands. Huge fangs lined the dinosaurs' mighty jaws.

▲ Tyrannosaurus, the most famous of the big meat eaters, was up to 41 ft. (12.4m) long.

▲ At 30 ft. (9m) long, Albertosaurus was much smaller than its relative Tyrannosaurus.

▲ Tarbosaurus was the biggest ever land-based hunter in Asia at 33 ft. (10m) long.

▲ No other predator in Late Cretaceous South America dared take on the massive, 43-ft. (13-m)-long Giganotosaurus.

GIANT DAGGER TEETH

Long, curved, flat teeth (right) at the sides of the dinosaurs' jaws had jagged edges. These teeth were ideal for slicing meat off an animal that was already dead. The dinosaurs may have used the shorter, thicker teeth at the front of their mouths to clamp into prey and stop it from escaping.

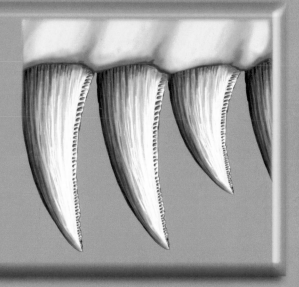

Creative corner

Make a Tyrannosaurus tooth
Shape a tooth in oven-bake modeling clay, using one of the teeth on p. 136 as a guide. Ask an adult to bake the tooth for you. Then paint it to look like the real thing.

◄ It is difficult to tell whether the meat that the large dinosaurs ate came from animals that they hunted for themselves or dead animals that they found. They all had the teeth of killers, but their size suggests that they were too big for chasing down fast-running prey.

The king

The most famous dinosaur that ever lived is Tyrannosaurus. This giant, 26-ft. (8-m)-tall carnivore stalked herds of plant eaters in Late Cretaceous North America. It picked on old, sick, or young animals that became separated from the others. Dead animals that it found along the way also fed its enormous appetite.

TYRANNOSAURUS SKIN?

This skin fossil belongs to a relative of Tyrannosaurus called Carnotaurus. The fossil shows that the dinosaur had very raised, knobby scales. It is possible that Tyrannosaurus's scales looked like this.

◄ We do not know the color of Tyrannosaurus. But experts think it blended in with its natural surroundings. This is why Tyrannosaurus models are often painted in the greens and browns of the dinosaur's forest habitat.

▼ Scientists who have studied bones and joints of Tyrannosaurus skeletons believe that the dinosaur was a slow mover. This is why many experts think that the dinosaur scavenged dead carcasses and preyed on vulnerable herd animals.

WHERE IS TYRANNOSAURUS FOUND TODAY?

Its fossils are found in rocks in North America. The biggest assembled skeleton is on display in the Field Museum in Chicago, Illinois.

▶ A Tyrannosaurus's skull was almost half as long as its body. This giant predator needed to have very strong muscles in its neck to support the weight of such an enormous head.

THE NAME

Tyrannosaurus is also known by its longer name, Tyrannosaurus rex. "Tyranno" means "tyrant," which is a cruel ruler, and "rex" means "king." Its name suits it well, as Tyrannosaurus was probably one of the largest and most terrifying carnivores around.

AMAZING!

Tyrannosaurus's brain was huge. But this dinosaur was probably not very smart—the thinking part of its brain was relatively tiny. Most of Tyrannosaurus's brain was for sight, smell, and controlling movement. These features of the brain helped it find and catch the food it needed to survive.

INTERNET LINKS: www.bbc.co.uk/nature/life/Tyrannosaurus

Duck-billed dinosaurs

In the Late Cretaceous, the most common plant-eating dinosaurs had wide, flattened snouts that resembled ducks' bills, or beaks. These duck-billed dinosaurs usually lived in herds. Many of them had eye-catching crests on their heads. They also had hundreds of teeth.

▼ The crests were made up of tubes that connected the throat and nose. The dinosaurs may have forced air through the tubes to make a noise like a trombone.

▶ Herds of different types of duck-billed dinosaurs probably fed side by side, a little like African antelope today. The dinosaurs returned to the same place every year to lay their eggs.

VOCABULARY

antelope
A fast-running, deerlike mammal with upward-pointing horns. Antelopes live in Africa and Asia.

communicate
To share information with others.

WHY DO WE THINK THE CRESTS MADE SOUNDS?

Scientists made models of the crests and then blew air through the nose. Each different shape made a different sound come out through the mouth.

CREST SHAPES

Each species of duck-billed dinosaur had its own style of head crest. It is likely that the different shapes produced different honking sounds. Scientists believe that the dinosaurs used these sounds to communicate with members of their own herd.

Parasaurolophus

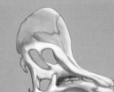

Corythosaurus

Lambeosaurus

Edmontosaurus

Bottom jaw

◀ Duck-billed dinosaurs had up to 500 teeth on each side of their top and bottom jaws. The teeth were tightly packed in rows. These panels of teeth were good for chewing tough plants.

INTERNET LINKS: www.nps.gov/akso/ParkWise/Students/ReferenceLibrary/Paleontology/Hadrosaurs.htm

Dinosaur babies

Like most reptiles today, dinosaurs reproduced by laying eggs. The eggs protected the young dinosaurs inside and provided them with food. There is evidence that some dinosaurs laid their eggs in nests and took care of their young. Several dinosaur nesting sites have been found. One of these is a nesting colony of Maiasaura in Montana.

EGG THIEF?

Oviraptor's name means "egg thief." It got this name because the first skeleton found seemed to be raiding a nest of Protoceratops eggs. But in the 1990s, another skeleton was found sitting on a nest of these eggs. They had been Oviraptor eggs all the time!

▲ Some of the Montana nests contained fossilized twigs, berries, and other parts of plants. These dinosaurs were herbivores, so it seems that the parents brought food to the nest for their babies.

◀ The Maiasaura nests in Montana show signs that they were dug out and repaired year after year. This suggests that the Maiasaura herd kept returning to the same nesting site when it was time to breed.

INTERNET LINKS: http://montanakids.com/history_and_prehistory/dinosaurs/maiasaur.htm

Spikes and clubs

Armored dinosaurs were a common sight in the Late Cretaceous, mostly on the continents of Asia, North America, and Europe. Some of the armored dinosaurs had all-over armor, with studs and spikes. Some even had bony clubs at the end of their tail.

▶ Edmontonia used its huge size and body armor to defend itself against predators such as Albertosaurus. The 20-ft. (6-m)-long armored dinosaur had spikes sticking out of its shoulders, sides, and tail.

VOCABULARY

club
A heavy stick that is thicker at one end. Some are used as weapons.

trot
To move at a pace that is faster than walking but slower than running.

CLUB TAIL
Bony lumps at the end of Euoplocephalus's tail created the club shape. The tip was about 3 ft. (1m) wide and was very heavy. It could probably break a predator's leg with a single swipe.

◀ Euoplocephalus was about 20 ft. (6m) long and weighed up to 2 tons. It could break into a trot if it had to, but running away was not this dinosaur's best defense. As well as its body armor, Euoplocephalus had its heavy tail club for protection.

▼ Not all of the Late Cretaceous armored dinosaurs were huge. Struthiosaurus was about the size of a sheep. It lived on islands off southeast Europe during the very end of the Cretaceous period.

Horned dinosaurs

Bulky, four-legged dinosaurs with large horns and spectacular neck frills were roaming North America in the Late Cretaceous. The horns and frills made these beasts look very frightening. But they actually spent most of their time grazing quietly. Their curved beaks were perfect for snipping vegetation.

▼ The dinosaurs probably used their horns to defend themselves against predators. Rival males may also have used their horns when they fought for mates during the mating season.

VOCABULARY

frill
A horned dinosaur's frill is the large leaf-shaped bone that surrounds its head.

mating season
A certain time in the year when animals come together to produce young.

▼ Each horned dinosaur species had its own style of frill and arrangement of horns. Triceratops (left) had three horns. Pachyrhinosaurus (middle) and Styracosaurus (right) had more than this.

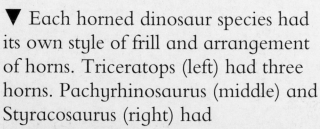

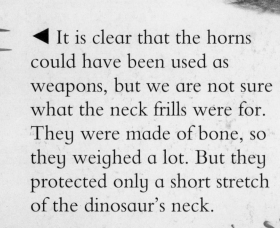

◀ It is clear that the horns could have been used as weapons, but we are not sure what the neck frills were for. They were made of bone, so they weighed a lot. But they protected only a short stretch of the dinosaur's neck.

Creative corner

Make a horned-dinosaur mask

(1) Cut out face and horn shapes from cardboard using this pattern as a guide. (2) Stick the horns onto the nose and forehead areas of the mask. (3) Add an elastic strap or ribbon to the back of the mask to keep it in place when you wear it. (4) Paint your mask.

1. Cut out

2. Add horns

3. Add strap

4. Paint

INTERNET LINKS: www.amnh.org/exhibitions/dinosaurs/display/horned.php

Triceratops

The most famous of all the horned dinosaurs is Triceratops. This large beast grew to 33 ft. (10m) long and weighed about 10 tons. Triceratops lived and traveled in herds. The adults may have worked together to defend themselves and their young from meat eaters.

▼ Herds of Triceratops probably trudged long distances in search of good grazing grounds. It was safer for them to travel in herds because a predator would find it difficult to single out one animal for slaughter.

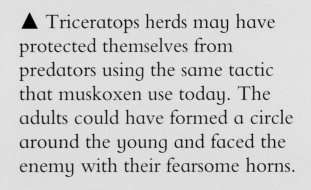

VOCABULARY

muskoxen
Large mammals with long, shaggy fur and curved horns.

slaughter
To kill an animal.

▲ Triceratops herds may have protected themselves from predators using the same tactic that muskoxen use today. The adults could have formed a circle around the young and faced the enemy with their fearsome horns.

WHAT DOES THE NAME "TRICERATOPS" MEAN?

It means "three-horned face." Triceratops had two horns on its forehead and one on its nose—that makes three!

▶ Triceratops was built like a rhinoceros, but it was twice the size of any rhinoceros living today. The dinosaur had a powerful neck and strong, sturdy legs so that it could carry its huge head.

INTERNET LINKS: www.childrenmuseum.org/themuseum/dinosphere/profiles/kelsey.html

The last dinosaurs

The dinosaurs were going strong at the end of the Cretaceous. We know this from fossil evidence found in rocks that formed at the time. Younger rocks that sit directly above the Cretaceous ones do not contain dinosaur fossils. This means that the dinosaurs were wiped out suddenly by something out of the ordinary.

▼ The Hell Creek rock formation in northern United States formed just before the dinosaurs died out. These are some of the dinosaurs found there.

▼ A larger variety of dinosaurs is found in Hell Creek than at any other site in the world. Triceratops is the most common dinosaur dug up there.

▲ Ankylosaurus fossils are rare at Hell Creek. This may be because these dinosaurs lived in places where their remains were less likely to be preserved.

CAN YOU FIND?
1. A Tyrannosaurus biting a duck-billed dinosaur
2. A Triceratops running

► Pachycephalosaurus lived in upland areas in North America before it was wiped out. This plant eater may have used its thick skull to head-butt rival males.

▼ Edmontosaurus's good eyesight, hearing, and sense of smell may have helped it avoid predators. Nothing could save this dinosaur from whatever wiped out all of the dinosaurs, though.

◄ Tyrannosaurus fossils are found in various levels of Late Cretaceous rocks. The Tyrannosaurus in the top level are the ones that died with all the other dinosaurs.

▲ The Struthiomimus that lived at Hell Creek were bigger than the ones found in other parts of North America. Maybe scientists will decide they are a different species.

INTERNET LINKS: www.youtube.com/watch?v=Gdh_3mLq80g

Impact!

The dinosaurs disappeared about 65 million years ago. Scientists are not sure what happened. Most think that a giant asteroid crashed into Earth, sending up huge clouds of dust. The scientists think that the dust blocked out light and warmth from the Sun for several years. Other scientists have different ideas.

WHAT IS AN ASTEROID?

An asteroid is a giant rock that drifts in space. They rarely strike Earth. Scientists can predict when and where they will hit.

▶ An asteroid would have killed everything that it struck. It could have caused forest fires that would have wiped out even more plants and animals. Dust carried on the winds could have choked to death many of the animals that had escaped the impact and fires.

◀ Some scientists think that erupting volcanoes were the cause of the extinction. Many volcanoes erupting at the same time could have created the same effects as an asteroid strike.

SURVIVORS

We can see descendants of survivors of the Late Cretaceous extinction living today. Turtles still swim in the seas. Tuatara, which are related to lizards and snakes, are members of a family that evolved at the time of the dinosaurs.

Green turtle

Tuatara

◀ With dust blotting out the Sun for years, Earth would have been plunged into freezing darkness. Species that could not cope with the new climate conditions would have become extinct.

▶ Another idea is that mammals killed off the dinosaurs by eating their eggs. Mammals certainly took advantage of the dinosaurs' bad luck—mammals have dominated Earth since the dinosaurs died out.

INTERNET LINKS: www.bbc.co.uk/nature/life/Dinosaur#p0014mdl

Now you know!

◀ A fossil unearthed in the Mongol Desert shows a Velociraptor and Protoceratops locked in a fight.

▲ Troodon had a large brain relative to its size, so this meat-eating dinosaur was probably more intelligent than many other dinosaurs.

▲ Tyrannosaurus had long, flat, jagged-edged teeth that ran along the sides of its jaws. They were the ideal shape for slicing into animal flesh.

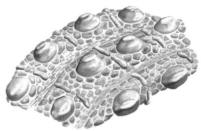

▲ It is likely that the skin of Tyrannosaurus was knobby and scaly like this.

▲ Certain duck-billed dinosaurs may have been able to force air through their crests to make noises.

◀ Horned dinosaurs probably used their horns to defend themselves against their enemies. We are not sure what their frills were for.

◀ Triceratops was one of the last dinosaurs that lived on Earth.

▶ An asteroid that crashed into Earth about 65 million years ago could have caused the extinction of the dinosaurs.

Dinosaur names

Dinosaurs and other prehistoric creatures have long Greek or Latin names that can be hard to say. Use this guide to find out how to pronounce the names of all the dinosaurs and other prehistoric animals in this book.

aetosaur (a-eat-oh-sor)

Albertosaurus (al-bert-oh-sor-us)

Allosaurus (al-oh-sor-us)

Alocodon (a-lok-oh-don)

Amphicoelias (am-fi-see-lee-as)

Ankylosaurus (an-kie-loh-sor-us)

Antarctosaurus
(ant-ark-toe-sor-us)

Apatosaurus (ah-pat-oh-sor-us)

Archaeopteryx (ark-ee-op-ter-ix)

Archaeoraptor (ark-ee-oh-rap-tor)

Archelon (ark-uh-lon)

archosaur (ark-oh-sor)

Argentinosaurus
(ar-gent-ee-no-sor-us)

Askeptosaurus
(ah-skep-toe-sor-us)

Atlascopcosaurus
(at-las-kop-kuh-sor-us)

Bambiraptor (bam-bee-rap-tor)

Baryonyx (bar-ee-on-ix)

Brachiosaurus
(brak-ee-oh-sor-us)

Brontosaurus (bron-toe-sor-us)

Bruhathkayosaurus
(brew-hath-kah-yo-sor-us)

Carnotaurus (car-noh-tor-us)

Caudipteryx (caw-dip-ter-ix)

Cearadactylus
(see-ah-rah-dak-til-us)

Ceratosaurus (seh-rat-oh-sor-us)

Cetiosaurus (see-tee-oh-sor-us)

Chaoyangsaurus
(chow-yang-sor-us)

Clevosaurus (clee-vo-sor-us)

Coelophysis (seel-oh-fie-sis)

Compsognathus
(komp-sog-nath-us)

Confuciusornis
(con-few-shus-or-nis)

Corythosaurus (co-rith-oh-sor-us)

crocodylomorph
(croc-oh-dil-oh-morf)

Cryolophosaurus
(cry-oh-lof-oh-sor-us)

Cryptoclidus (crip-toe-clide-us)

Ctenochasma (sten-oh-kazz-mah)

cynodonts (si-noh-donts)

Dacentrurus (dah-sen-troo-russ)

Deinocheirus (die-no-kie-russ)

Deinonychus (die-non-ie-kuss)

diapsid (die-ap-sid)

Dilong (die-long)

Dilophosaurus
(die-loaf-oh-sor-us)

Dimorphodon (die-morf-oh-don)

Diplodocus (dip-lod-oh-kuss)

Dryosaurus (dry-oh-sor-us)

Dsungaripterus
(jung-ah-rip-ter-us)

Edmontonia (ed-mon-toe-nee-ah)

Edmontosaurus
(ed-mon-toe-sor-us)

Elaphrosaurus (el-laf-roe-sor-us)

Elasmosaurus
(el-lazz-moe-sor-us)

Eoraptor (ee-oh-rap-tor)

Euoplocephalus
(you-op-luh-sef-ah-lus)

Eustreptospondylus
(you-strep-toe-spon-die-luss)

Fabrosaurus (fab-ro-sor-us)

Geosaurus (jee-oh-sor-us)

Giganotosaurus
(jee-ga-no-toe-sor-us)

Giraffatitan (ji-raf-ah-tie-tan)

Glacialisaurus
(glay-see-al-ih-sor-us)

Herrerasaurus
(huh-rare-uh-sor-us)

Heterodontosaurus
(het-er-oh-dont-oh-sor-us)

Huayangosaurus
(hwah-yang-oh-sor-us)

Hypsilophodon (hip-sill-oh-foe-don)

ichthyosaur (ik-thee-oh-sor)

Iguanodon (ig-wan-oh-don)

Incisivosaurus
(in-size-ih-voh-sor-us)

Juralibellula (Jur-ah-li-bell-you-la)

Kentrosaurus (ken-troh-sor-us)

Kuehneosaurus
(cune-ee-oh-sor-us)

Kuehneotherium
(cune-ee-oh-theer-ee-um)

Lambeosaurus

(lam-bee-oh-sor-us)

Leaellynasaura (lee-el-in-ah-sor-ah)

lepidosaur (leh-pid-oh-sor)

Lesothosaurus (le-so-toe-sor-us)

Liopleurodon (lie-oh-ploor-oh-don)

Lourinhanosaurus

(loh-rin-hah-noh-sor-us)

Lufengosaurus

(loo-fung-oh-sor-us)

Maiasaura (my-ah-sor-uh)

Marasuchus (mah-rah-soo-kuss)

marginocephalian

(mahr-gin-oh-sef-fay-lee-an)

Massospondylus

(mass-oh-spon-dih-luss)

Megalosaurus

(meg-uh-low-sor-us)

Mei (may)

Metriorhynchus (met-ree-oh-rin-kus)

Microraptor (mike-roh-rap-tor)

Miragaia (mere-ah-gai-ah)

mosasaur (moes-ah-sor)

Mussaurus (moo-sor-us)

Nothosaurus (no-tho-sor-us)

Ophthalmosaurus

(off-thal-mow-sor-us)

ornithischian (or-neh-thisk-ee-en)

Ornithocheirus (or-nith-oh-care-us)

Ornitholestes (or-nith-oh-les-teez)

ornithopod (or-nith-oh-pod)

Ornithosuchidae

(or-nith-oh-soo-ki-die)

Ouranosaurus

(ooh-ran-oh-sor-us)

Oviraptor (oh-vih-rap-tore)

Pachycephalosaurus

(pack-ee-cef-al-oh-sor-us)

Pachyrhinosaurus

(pack-ee-rine-oh-sor-us)

Parasaurolophus

(par-ah-sor-oh-loh-fus)

phytosaur (fie-toe-sor)

Placodus (plack-oh-dus)

Plateosaurus (plat-ee-oh-sor-us)

plesiosaur (plee-see-oh-sor)

pliosaurs (ply-oh-sor)

Protarchaeopteryx

(pro-tark-ee-op-ter-ix)

Protoceratops (pro-toe-ser-a-tops)

Protosuchus (pro-toe-soo-kuss)

Pterodactylus (terr-oh-dak-til-us)

Pterodaustro (teh-roe-daw-stroh)

pterosaur (terr-oh-sor)

Quetzalcoatlus

(kwet-zal-koh-at-lus)

rauisuchian (raw-i-soo-ki-an)

Rhamphorhynchus (ram-fo-rin-kus)

rhynchosaur (rin-ko-sor)

Rutiodon (roo-tie-oh-don)

Saltasaurus (salt-ah-sor-us)

saurischian (saw-ris-key-en)

sauropod (saw-roh-pod)

Sauroposeidon (sor-oh-po-sie-don)

Saurosuchus (sor-oh-soo-kuss)

Scelidosaurus

(skel-ih-doh-sor-us)

Scutellosaurus

(scoo-tel-oh-sor-us)

Segnosaurus (seg-no-sor-us)

Shastasaurus (sha-sta-sor-us)

Shunosaurus (shoon-oh-sor-us)

Sinornithosaurus

(sine-or-nith-oh-sor-us)

Sinosauropteryx

(sine-oh-sor-op-ter-ix)

Sinovenator (sine-oh-ven-a-tor)

Staurikosaurus (stor-ik-oh-sor-us)

stegosaur (steg-oh-sor)

Stegosaurus (steg-oh-sor-us)

Struthiomimus

(struth-ee-oh-mime-us)

Styracosaurus (sty-rak-oh-sor-us)

Suchomimus (soo-ko-mime-us)

Supersaurus (soo-per-sor-us)

Syntarsus (sin-tar-sus)

Tapejara (tap-eh-har-ah)

Tarbosaurus (tar-bo-sor-us)

Tenontosaurus

(ten-on-toe-sor-us)

tetanuran (te-tan-ooh-ran)

Thecodontosaurus

(thee-co-don-toe-sor-us)

Therizinosaurus

(thair-ih-zeen-oh-sor-us)

theropod (ther-oh-pod)

thyreophoran

(thy-re-oh-for-an)

Timimus (tih-mime-us)

Torvosaurus (tor-voh-sor-us)

Triceratops (tri-ser-a-tops)

trilobite (tri-low-bite)

Troodon (true-oh-don)

Typothorax (tie-po-thor-ax)

Tyrannosaurus

(tie-ran-oh-sor-us)

Velociraptor (vell-oss-ih-rap-tor)

Xiaosaurus (she-ow-sor-us)

Yangchuanosaurus

(yang-choo-ah-no-sor-us)

Index

Acknowledgments

The publisher would like to thank the following illustrators from Linden Artists:
Adam Hook, Stuart Lafford, Patricia Ludlow, Shane Marsh, Sebastian Quigley, Sam Weston

All "Creative corner" illustrations by Ray Bryant

DISCARD